ENDORSEMENTS

Pastor Judy Jacobs has presented a revelation and challenge to every Christian to pray until we appropriate the promises of God. It is not a revelation without reality. Judy demonstrates that revelation is not just ideas in the mind, for she paid the price to prove that it works. The Body of Christ will be more victorious and productive by reading and practicing the truths in this book.

BISHOP BILL HAMON
Christian International Apostolic-Global Network

Pray Until is the trajectory shift you have been praying for. Judy Jacobs has painted us a brilliant picture of how to receive our miracles. God has already done the miracle for you—now walk in it. This is your "how to" book. This is a must read!

"Real Talk" KIM JONES
Senior Pastor, Limitless Church

Pastor Judy Jacobs is a mighty woman of God with a life-changing ministry. I am honored to call her a covenant friend, and I am excited to see her bring this inspiring message of hope, *Pray Until*, to Christians around the world! I truly believe that when you read this book and apply its principles, there is no limit to what God will do in and through you!

PASTOR CANDY CHRISTMAS
Regeneration Church
Nashville, Tennessee

Judy Jacobs has done it again, like only she can, and has put words to paper that so clearly capture what the Body of Christ needs to hear right now! Her new book *Pray Until* is a life-changer if you'll apply the message to your life!

Tony Suarez

RevivalMakers

www.tonysuarez.com

Judy Jacobs never ceases to inspire us to press in to possess our promised breakthrough. *Pray Until* will fire up your prayer life with persistence, power, and possibilities. You will refer to it again and again to find the courage to fight and win!

Jane Hamon

Vision Church @ Christian International

Author: *Dreams & Visions, The Deborah Company,*

Discernment & Declarations for Breakthrough

PRAY

Until

THE SECRET TO RECEIVING YOUR MIRACLE

JUDY JACOBS

DESTINY IMAGE® PUBLISHERS, INC.

P.O. Box 310, Shippensburg, PA 17257-0310

"Promoting Inspired Lives."

This book and all other Destiny Image and Destiny Image Fiction books are available at Christian bookstores and distributors worldwide.

For more information on foreign distributors, call 717-532-3040.

Reach us on the Internet: www.destinyimage.com.

ISBN 13 TP: 978-0-7684-6309-5
ISBN 13 eBook: 978-0-7684-6310-1
ISBN 13 HC: 978-0-7684-6312-5
ISBN 13 LP: 978-0-7684-6311-8

For Worldwide Distribution, Printed in the U.S.A.

1 2 3 4 5 6 7 8 / 26 25 24 23 22

DEDICATION

I dedicate this book to my forever friend and husband of almost 30 years. Our faith, determination, and perseverance got us through one of the roughest times of our little family's life. Thank you for being the king, prophet, and priest when I needed it so desperately. Also, our "sugar-bear" who was the stabilizer for all of us, especially Kaylee. Thank you, Erica, for just being your incredible self, always!

I dedicate this book to my amazing mom, Gaynell Chavis Jacobs, who had me at the ripe ole age of 46, and who taught all her children to *pray until*. It won't be long before we are all united. Praise God!

My brother, Roger, who was there to help me with my first "baby blue." My sister, Sylvia, who kept her promise to my mom to look after my brother Jerry when he was so far from God and a life of stability. You did awesome!

I dedicate this book to my girl, Judith Kaylee, who bears my name, and her grandmother, Parmalee. Sweetheart, there are no words to describe how very God-proud Dad and I are of all your accomplishments that you have done and especially what is yet to be. We were there in the beginning, but you and God took the reins and today your testimony is a dagger in the heart of your enemy. Can't wait to see what's ahead!

Finally, I dedicate this book to our Lord and Savior who proved faithful to do what He says He will do.

Now to those who are still believing—*Pray Until!*

Acknowledgments

I love the household of faith because they are in actuality the Body of Christ that helps us all to function in the Kingdom of God.

This project is a testimony of the people of God who help to advance the Kingdom of God. Psalm 68:11 confirms it by saying, *"The Lord gave the word: great was the company of those that published it."*

My deepest appreciation to Larry Sparks and Destiny Image Publishers for allowing for this revelation to be published. May Christ be magnified even greater.

To the editors for your hard work to make sure everything is completed in excellence.

My heartfelt thanks for my friend, Karen Wheaton for your beautiful contribution to the Foreword and for your amazing "yes" to Jesus to change a generation, and you have—including our two daughters.

Thank you to our families (Jacobs and Tuttles) who have been there to encourage and support us every step of the way.

My covenant friend, Kathie Kennemer, a pre-editor elitist, prayer partner, and a true lover of Jesus.

A special thank you to Pastor Kent and Candy Christmas for giving support to continue the incredible legacy of Pastor Joshua Christmas. May many lives and hearts be delivered and set free.

My heartfelt thanks to Pastor Josh and Nadine Bowles for sharing with the world the incredible miracle of Sammy!

Our beautiful Dwelling Place Church family for being the support you are week in and week out. You are our why!

A very special thank you to Heather Jewitt, our dedicated administrative pastor, office manager, my on-the-road travel partner, and especially my friend. May your reward be great to you and your family here and there!

The deposit that Lari and Carolyn Goss made in our lives is incalculable on this planet, but one day soon we will all know.

A big shout-out to those church mamas mentioned, and so many more, who forever marked my life.

Contents

FOREWORD

*I*f I am going into an active war zone to take a front-line position, I would prefer to fight beside a soldier who has been well trained, fully given, strong and brave, and determined to win—no matter the cost. Many years ago, God placed beside me that kind of soldier. Her name is Judy Jacobs.

We met on the battlefield—a spiritual battlefield, that is. Although often assigned to different posts, each of us has traveled around the world, carrying the message our Father gave us to deliver. Whether we traveled separately or stood side by side, we have always shared the same heart and passion for the mission we have been called to carry out.

I remember well one day in particular when Judy called me. The battle had hit close to home. Judy was in serious conflict with an enemy that was seeking to destroy the life and purpose of her daughter, Kaylee. I could hear it in her voice—the urgency, the desperation, but most of all the resolve. She spoke with shameless determination and targeted faith as she declared to me, "Karen, I need you to stand with me, now! The enemy has attacked Kaylee. I am in the fight of my life. But I will not give up until I win."

We prayed. We stood. We believed, we saw God break through with a mighty victory over the hideous enemy that had attacked Kaylee's life.

Little did I know only a few short years later this scenario would be played out again, only this time I was the one calling on Judy to fight with me for my youngest daughter, Lindsey.

I found myself engaged in the greatest battle of spiritual warfare I had ever experienced. As the battle erupted, I knew I could not fight this one alone. I remembered my friend, my comrade. I picked up the phone and called Judy.

"Judy, I need help. I need you now to stand with me! We have to fight and win for Lindsey."

During this season of intercession, Judy not only preached to me but she exemplified the message of this book: *Pray Until*! The revelation of that simple word has changed my life forever.

This book is not for the fainthearted, but neither is the battlefield. All of us are at war for our children, our marriages, our health, our nation, and even our very lives. We have to choose whether we will give up and allow the enemy to prevail in his plan to steal, kill, and destroy. Or we can choose to stand and fight! However, you must remember you cannot fight this battle alone. You need someone to stand with you, to encourage you, and to believe with you until your promised victory is fully manifested.

That is why you are holding this book. This is no ordinary book; it is a friend. Judy Jacobs is not only "my" comrade in battle; today, she has become yours. As you are reading the pages of this book, listen carefully and you will hear Judy's voice shouting to you in the middle of your battlefield. "Keep on fighting! Keep on praying! We will not stop—*until! Until!*"

KAREN WHEATON
Founder of The Ramp
theramp.org

INTRODUCTION

$\mathcal{J}$ohn Wesley said, "God will do nothing on earth except in answer to believing prayer."

The two key words here are *believing prayer*. Hebrews 11:6 gives the key to believing prayer: "*for he that cometh to God must believe that he is, and that he is a rewarder of them that diligently seek him.*"

I believe this book holds the *secret* to receiving your miracle from God for those who pray believing prayers or, as I want to say in this book, for those who *Pray Until*. Jeremiah reminds us of this secret ingredient: "*Call unto me, and I will answer thee, and show thee great and mighty things, which thou knowest not*" (Jer. 33:3).

That's the secret! Calling unto Him! When we call on the Lord Jesus, He hears. Solomon said it is the glory of God to conceal a matter, but the glory of kings to search out a matter (see Prov. 25:2).

I believe the revelation that is in this book will help you to search out the things in your life that matter—the things you are praying your *until prayer* for, believing they will be answered!

Dr. Jack Hayford gives a great response in his book on prayer along the lines of John Wesley's admonition:

3

He still holds to His original proposition: "Man is in charge on earth. If hell is allowed to take over, or if the flesh fumbles the ball, it's man's duty to call upon Me for the remedy. If he doesn't call—if prayer isn't uttered—I have bound Myself not to be involved. If prayer is extended, I have bound Myself to conquer everything that would destroy or diminish My beloved creature, man."

There it is.

Prayer can change anything.

The impossible doesn't exist.

His is the power.

Ours is the prayer.

Without Him, we cannot.

Without us, He will not.[1]

As you are reading this book, I believe that God is granting you the wisdom, the insight, and the revelation to not only search out matters in your life but to find the answers that you have been looking for. Jesus said, "*Ask, and it shall be given you; seek, and ye shall find; knock, and it shall be opened unto you*" (Matt. 7:7). When you become desperate, you will go to any degree to search out a thing and to see something change in your life.

Desperation does some really interesting and extraordinary things in an individual. It systematically causes the real you to come out when you are facing situations in the spirit or in the flesh that are not pleasant or are painful and unexpected. If you're reading this book, you are more than likely facing an ordeal that compelled you to pick it up. Maybe it's because you really do find yourself in a desperate place.

For example, when you're desperate to lose weight, you will try every fad diet known to man. You will exercise, join a gym, and even order the latest and greatest craze product available. You do that because you are desperate to fit into those jeans from ten years ago. When you're desperate for your marriage to last and not end in divorce, you will go the extra mile—and you should, because you're so desperate and your marriage matters!

Sometimes desperation as a parent causes you to give in to a child and play the role of an enabler instead of blocking those things you know are causing more harm than good. Quite frankly, deep down in your knower, you know it needs to stop. Your head says, "Just give them what they want, and they will be happy." But deep down, as a mother, father, brother, sister, or friend, you know you're contributing to their demise. What is the answer? What can get you to the other side of this thing facing your marriage? How can you see your child set free? What is the secret to your household salvation? One word—*until!*

Every person who goes through this thing called life will face an *until moment* in their prayer life, family, marriage, body, and other areas that you are believing God for. What will decide the outcome of your decision will be your tenacity to believe God and to stay focused on your *until.* Praying *until!* Believing *until!* Staying *until!* Standing *until!* Declaring *until!* Until when, Judy? Until you get your prayer answered, of course.

I love to read and write about life experiences. Life experiences are common and, consequently, also very personal, challenging, and compelling. There is no cheating because when you encounter life, it hits you head-on and usually right between the eyes, but on the other side of these life experiences there are great testimonies of victory, power, and change!

That victory, power, and change will come through something that we live by every single day of our lives, and that is faith. Growing up, my parents taught me that faith is something very sure, solid, and true. It is not a fairy tale. Faith is something you hook yourself up to and become rooted and grounded in the truth of what the Bible teaches you that faith is. I have found out in my life experiences that the more truth and steadfastness you have, the more true and steadfast you will be. The more stable and grounded your faith becomes, the more stable and grounded you will become. In essence, faith causes you to become strong in every area of your life. Such is the revelation that I will share with you in these pages to come. They are raw, telling, informative, and I know they will help you to become more grounded and stable. My prayer is that it will be life-changing to those who are waiting for their prayer to be answered!

The Bible states in Deuteronomy 29:29, "*The secret things belong to the Lord our God, but the things revealed belong to us and to our children forever*" (NIV). There absolutely are some things that only the Father knows, such as the second return of our Lord and Savior, Jesus Christ. Matthew 24:36 emphatically states, "*But about that day or hour no one knows, not even the angels in heaven, nor the Son, but only the Father*" (NIV).

So the secret things belong to God. He knows things about all of us, and yet He chooses not to reveal those things, and maybe we're better off because of it. However, there are some things that I believe that the Father *wants* us to know! There is so much more that has to be discovered because:

Eye hath not seen, nor ear heard, neither have entered into the heart of man, the things which God hath prepared for them that love him (1 Corinthians 2:9).

The whole entire Bible is chock-full of things that are waiting to be revealed. Here's what I know—if God says that something belongs to me, then I want all that God has ordained for me and my children and their children to come. We are to pass on to our children all the blessings, promises, and guarantees that were written for them and for us.

Read the words found in this book because I know they work. This revelation worked for me; as a matter of fact, it is still working, and I believe it will work for you as well. It is the secret to getting all that you desire from your heavenly Father who desires to bless you more than you can get your mind to believe. Your *until* is waiting on the other side of a decision to seek God in a manner you never knew possible because you have never been this desperate before. Prayer will become your brand-new language. The Word will become what you eat, sleep, and drink!

This book, along with the Word of the Lord, will be your go-to, your catalyst, your catapult, and your courage to trust God when everything in life screams *give up!* You *will* get to the other side of this thing, for with God there is never an *if*—there is always a *when!* But your *when* determines your *until!* So come with me on this quest of expectation. I am believing as you read these words, life and light will illuminate your heart, your mind, *and* your situation, along with your faith. These precious truths will converge to see the greatest miracle you have ever experienced!

I invite you to *pray until!*

Note

1. Jack Hayford, *Prayer Is Invading the Impossible* (Newberry, FL: Bridge-Logos Publishers, 1977), 97.

PERSPECTIVE

*J*eremiah 29:11-13 in The Message says, *"I know what I'm doing. I have it all planned out—plans to take care of you, not abandon you, plans to give you the future you hope for. When you call on me, when you come and pray to me, I'll listen. When you come looking for me, you'll find me."*

I've heard and known this scripture most of my life; I've quoted it many times and shared it when others needed to be encouraged. However, I had never really had to literally apply it until Judy and I faced a very demonic uphill battle with our daughter Kaylee. You'll read her powerful story in the chapters to come. In that season, as a father, I was holding on to or grabbing anything that spoke encouragement and hope to such a hopeless situation. As men do, and as a new father, I prided myself on being the one who was strong, in control, and could lead in overcoming this dire situation; however, inside I was struggling to find any answers for my wife and daughter; in my mind I was failing. Many days they would look so desperately to me and plead for answers for the fight.

Many times I would get in my car and just drive for hours, toiling over what to do. I even had the "where are You, God, are You even real" conversations with the Lord, while knowing in my heart He had to be in control or we would never make it. It was during those drives or long walks of questioning Him and longing to help Kaylee that I would hear Jeremiah 29:11-13 in my soul. Now this is a powerful scripture, and we all apply it to our lives, but in reality there is embedded in the words a process that must happen for such a future and hope to come to pass.

The process is never any fun, and yet it's leading to an anointed purpose and calling. *En route* to the promise, there are tests, challenges, and real demonic strategies to cause us to fail as parents, husbands, wives, or just believers in general. It's a death, a diagnosis, a child's struggles, a divorce, or just the 10,000-plus things in a hard-knock life that constantly push us to the end of our own sanity. However, the promises of God still stand, and His faithfulness to His perfect will for us shines through in every situation.

God challenges us to trust Him in the most devastating seasons, to seek Him when we don't know what to do. It's the hardest thing to do because we want to fix and heal it in the moment. Yet God is working, building, and preparing us for our future and the futures of our children. He is teaching us to pray like we've never prayed and fast until it hurts, while at the same time being relentless in our passionate pursuit of Him. In the end and on the other side of our worst battles, we find He was always watching over us, making a way where there is no way, and seeing to it that His plans are established for His glory and our good. The final result—we are stronger and victorious because of it. Hallelujah!

PASTOR JAMIE TUTTLE
Dwelling Place Church

Chapter 1

My Until Moment

So don't follow me without considering what it will cost you. For who would construct a house before first sitting down to estimate the cost to complete it? Otherwise he may lay the foundation and not be able to finish. The neighbors will ridicule him, saying, "Look at him! He started to build but couldn't complete it!" Have you ever heard of a commander who goes out to war without first sitting down with strategic planning to determine the strength of his army to win the war against a stronger opponent? If he knows he doesn't stand a chance of winning the war, the wise commander will send out delegates to ask for the terms of peace. Likewise, unless you surrender all to me, giving up all you possess, you cannot be one of my disciples.

—LUKE 14:28-33 TPT

When God sets His heart on you, you will be tried often. But the fact is, the longer and harder your affliction, the more deeply God has set His heart on you, to show you His love and care.

—DAVID WILKERSON

*P*astor Jack W. Hayford stated:

> Most of us don't pray on a regular basis because we're deeply aware that it will cost us something. More than time. More than money. More than faith. More than becoming religious. To lay hold of prayer as my own available resource for effective, practical, daily use...will cost me one thing. Honesty.[1]

I have always been one who is very interested in a price tag. You know what I'm talking about. It's that little tag that hangs under a blouse sleeve or the arm of a dress. My favorite is when they hide the price tag from you. You know this price is not on full display because the store only appeals to a certain clientele—people who are not interested in price tags. For the rest of us, they hide the price tag so that hopefully everybody won't walk out of the store at the same time because of how high the prices are. No matter where I shop or no matter what I'm shopping for, I always want to know, "What is the bottom line? Just give me the bottom line, please." That has always been my slogan. I just want to know, "What is this going to cost me?"

If I am flying across the country to minister in a church, concert, conference, or ministry venue, there are some very important details I will need to know before I leave home. Some of those questions would include, "What will be the timeline? When will I leave and when will I arrive? When can I expect to get back home?" The next question is obvious: "What is expected of me when I arrive at the destination? Is it just to sing, to preach and minister in the Word, or both?" How about this one: "How many times am

I asked to minister while I am out of town? How many venues or churches will I minister at while I am away? Will I be traveling to other places while I am there in this particular part of the country to minister as well?" These are all very legitimate questions that I face week in and week out as a minister of this glorious Gospel.

One of the most important commodities you possess is your time. What is it going to cost me to be a friend? What will it cost me to say yes to being on a particular committee? Or what will it cost me to marry this person? What is involved in being the parent of a child? How about this one—getting that little dog your kids are begging you for? (I personally know the cost of that one!) But here's the big one—what will it cost me to follow Jesus? I can tell you the answer to that one straight up. It will cost you *everything!*

Now let me ask you this question. What will it cost you to see your prayers answered? What will it cost to see your prodigal come home? A marriage restored? A miracle in your finances? Being delivered from a fear or an addiction? A healing in your body? What will it cost you to see that Jesus gets what He paid for? What will it cost you to see the face of Jesus and spend eternity with Him? Let me tell you what it will cost you—it will cost you your *until!*

As I began to contemplate writing this book, I knew the first thing that would be required of me is to show why *I* am qualified to write a book on "praying until." I will be quick to confess that waiting until anything is *not* one of my fortes, but it seems as if it is one of God's favorites in teaching His children discipline and spiritual maturity.

When I met my husband, Jamie, we were traveling with a recruitment group for a university. He was the drummer, and of course I was a vocalist. We dated four to five years off and on, and then we fell in love with each other and he asked me to marry him and I said, "*Yes!*" Little did I know what that yes would cost me, and us as a couple, and later on as a family.

We got married and began to travel all over the world. After four years, it was time to begin thinking about having a family, and we were excited at the very thought of it.

When we finally learned that we were pregnant there was so much joy within our families and our friends, and along with that came much celebration that a baby was on the way. Flowers filled the house, cards of congratulations came in the mail, and it seemed the whole world was in great anticipation of this baby that had been a long time coming for me. People had waited for me to find that person who would be my soul mate in marriage. At the age of 36 I found myself walking down the aisle of a church, and now the next best thing was on the way—a baby!

We waited for weeks before we were scheduled to go to the doctor to hear the baby's heartbeat for the first time. We truly were giddy. I remember thinking, "Oh, is this baby going to be a boy or a girl, a Tuttle or a Jacobs?" So many questions and such excitement we could hardly contain ourselves. When we finally got into the room to hear the heartbeat, nothing was happening. I was looking straight into the eyes of the nurse who was conducting the scan, but I noticed that she wouldn't look back at me. Jamie and I kept saying to her, "Is something wrong? What's going on?" She just kept scanning my tummy.

Finally, she excused herself and left the room and very soon afterward the doctor came in to do the evaluation of the scan himself. Then came the news: "I am sorry to tell you Mr. and Mrs. Tuttle, but there is no heartbeat."

After that statement, I really don't remember a whole lot that happened, except feeling like someone had hit me with a stun gun. The devastation that followed was probably one of the lowest points in my life to this day. The shock, the loss, the disillusionment—tears, tears, and more tears flowed uncontrollably. I could not believe this was happening to me. Not me! My mama had 15 children in all. Yes, there had been two miscarriages that she had suffered with, but those thoughts never entered my mind. Now here I was. I thought, *This is not supposed to happen to me! I pray for people who go through these things. No! Not me!*

The days after were tough days of trusting, denial, questioning, and, after a while, worshiping. One thing I know for sure is that the enemy is always after your seed, especially your first-fruit seed. He knows it is significant because it is the greatest strength of the father and the best part of the DNA of the mother and father combined. There is great promise in the first fruit, because in the Jewish culture the firstborn came with many responsibilities to carry on the given name and to represent the name, reputation, and spirit of the family. We felt cheated, but we knew that God was a Redeemer and a Restorer, so we chose to trust Him.

Those days were tough after the miscarriage. At times, I felt as if I would never recover from that incident, but we leaned heavily on the sovereignty of our Father and knew that He was in total control and that one day we would see our baby for the first time and be united forever.

As time passed, we became pregnant again and with great excitement our bouncing baby girl, Judith Kaylee, was born. She was born in August and I turned 40 in September of that same year. (By the way, I do not recommend that time frame for anyone at all!) Oh, what a happy day when our little princess came. We could hardly believe we were holding her in our arms. Just a little under 48 hours before, Jamie had gotten down on his knees and spoke to Kaylee in my tummy and announced to her, "KayKay, it's time for you to come because it is your due date." About two hours later, my water broke and we went to the hospital and around 11:52 p.m. on her due date, she was born! Oh what a jubilee!

After Kaylee came, almost three years later Erica Janell, our second baby girl, arrived. By this time, life was really popping, to say the least. It seemed as if the whole world was beckoning for us to come, come, come. So off we would go, go, go, with babies in tow. During most of the girls' young lives we had a wonderful caregiver, Eleanor, who would travel with us. Lots of times, we chose to let the girls stay at home, and Eleanor would stay in our home to take care of the girls so that they would always be in their familiar place. That was a wonderful blessing in all of our lives.

However, something began to happen when Kaylee was around seven or eight years old. While other young girls were freely skipping, playing, and laughing and making friends, Kaylee began to struggle and be very clingy and show signs of anxiety. We were concerned, especially because she didn't want to go to school. Knowing she had never been exposed to any kind of abuse or trauma, we came to the conclusion, through prayer, that this was a spirit of fear that had gripped our young baby girl's heart, and it was fierce. What came next was one of my reasons for writing this book and this revelation.

Life is sometimes defined by specific times and seasons. I have always tried to trust the Lord in the timelines of my life when it seemed as if I would never reach some life goals. As a young woman, I wanted to see some things accomplished in my life, such as graduating from college, getting married, having children, and traveling into every nation of the earth, and doing all of this at the same time. Looking back over the last decades of this journey, the seasons have been amazing, exhilarating, adventuresome, exhausting, and at times frightful. But without reservation I can declare that God has been faithful every step of the way.

My life has always been centered around the Word of the Lord. I have placed my trust in every single solitary verse since before I could read, and then my mama would read the Bible to all of us or we would sit in church and listen to the preacher as he proclaimed and taught the Word of the Lord. Believe me when I tell you, when I was in church I did listen, or else I would be escorted out with a specific intention in mind, or a very strong tapping on the head while sitting in front of my mama.

Throughout my young years going into my teenage and college years, there was one particular psalm that always stuck out in my mind. David said, *"I trust in you, Lord; I say, 'You are my God.' My times are in your hands"* (Ps. 31:14-15 NIV). David's son, Solomon, also had some things to say about time:

> *God has made everything beautiful for its own time. He has planted eternity in the human heart, but even so, people cannot see the whole scope of God's work from beginning to end* (Ecclesiastes 3:11 NLT).

Only God sees the end from the beginning. If you are stuck waiting in front of a railroad track as a train passes in front of you, car by car, you can't see the little caboose at the end that always indicates you will soon be moving. No! The only way to visibly see the end from the beginning is to be up in an airplane looking down. That way, you will see the big black engine at the front and the little red caboose at the very end. That is the way God sees our lives. He is the sovereign Father; He knows all, sees all, and He determines all. We just have to trust Him.

The timing of the Lord was everything for me in waiting on my *until* moment, and I can guarantee you this—your *until* moment will always involve waiting on the Lord's timing and *faithing it!*

The Bible has lots to say on prayer. I believe one of the strongest truths about prayer is that it brings you into a fellowship with your heavenly Father. Prayer is that unbroken communication between you and the lover of your soul. It's when all of Heaven recognizes there is something very precious going on so all of Heaven stops to hear the sincere soul-cry of God's child.

Jack Hayford says, "Prayer is invading the impossible." It is the language of Heaven that gets the ears of our Father God.

I love my brother-in-law, Wes Tuttle, who is a gifted songwriter. Wes has written many songs that I have recorded through the years, but I particularly love the song that he recorded simply entitled "Prayer," which uses the words of an old hymn penned by James Montgomery. Here are some of the lines:

> Prayer is the soul's sincere desire,
> uttered or unexpressed;
> the motion of a hidden fire
> that trembles in the breast.
> Prayer is the burden of a sigh,

the falling of a tear,

the upward glancing of an eye

when none but God is near.

Prayer is the Christian's vital breath,

the Christian's native air,

his watchword at the gates of death,

he enters Heaven with prayer.

Because Kaylee was being attacked with a devilish spirit of fear to torment and destroy her life, prayer now had to go up to another level that I had never known before. Here's what I know about prayer:

- Prayer is powerful.

- Prayer is active.

- Prayer moves, it shifts; it rattles the enemy, and it brings extraordinary change.

And depending on what you're praying about, it can either hold something back or pull something forward. But when you pray you have to be ready to persevere in prayer, encourage yourself, accompany it with violent faith, and you must contend and pray *until!*

Some words define us, making a difference in our lives forever. In our culture, church, and world, words easily evoke emotions. Words represent things, they convey certain ideas, they encourage us, they lift us, they build us up, and at the same time words can destroy and tear us down. The wrong words coming from a place of darkness, restlessness, and wandering can anger us, belittle us, destroy our self-esteem, and either bring life or bring death.

I love words. I don't study them as much as I want to, but I enjoy reading and I get great satisfaction from the cognitive process of understanding words and how they create and form thoughts.

Let's look at the definitions of this word *until*. It is really interesting to me how the dictionary defines the word *until* in all of its varied uses. The term is used in different settings:

- Up to the time of
- Before a specified time
- To the point in time, or, to the extent that something happens
- Onward to, or until an occurrence

Also, when using *until* as a preposition, you do something until or till a particular time, then you stop doing it at that time.

As long as I live, I will never forget how the revelation came for this book to be written and published. It was because of this one word I heard in my spirit one Monday morning. The word was *until!* I was upstairs in my room as usual, praying, waiting, and listening. All at once, something came over me and the only way I can explain it is to say it was an unction from the Holy Spirit. A holy fervor, a righteous indignation, rose up in me. I remember everyone was home that day because it was the beginning of summer, and I came to the conclusion that I couldn't take it anymore. I couldn't take what my baby was going through. And of course her daddy and sister and all of us around her were dealing with this spirit of fear on a daily basis.

It really dawned on me during prayer that day, "What will the enemy do with the word *until*?" I mean really, how can he possibly calibrate, turn it, or twist it in a way to get me to give up praying for my child? He can't! So how would he handle the word *until*? Oh! Now I was excited and fired up.

Jamie was downstairs with the girls, and I came down the stairs very emphatically and announced to my husband, to all of Heaven, and certainly to all of hell, "I am going on a fast!"

My husband looked at me and said, "Okay, I'll fast with you."

"That's fine," I said, "if you want to."

"Okay then, how long are we going to fast?" my husband asked.

I'm sure by now there was fire in my eyes and smoke coming from my ears. "Until!" I said.

"Until when? A week? Two weeks? How long can I expect?" Jamie responded. "I will have to make some arrangements."

I could hear the desperation coming from Jamie's voice. My unsettled feeling was rising as all of a sudden I made the announcement, "I am going to fast *until!* Until I see a change in my child's life! I am going to fast until I see victory and a difference that something has happened in her life!"

I never knew what that decision would cost me, nor did I realize the victory that would come. Though it was not easy, I knew from faith's standpoint the victory was already settled. I had to wait on the Lord!

Jamie and I began a fast that started out as a total fast for two weeks of nothing but water, then continued with many more fasts ahead—decreeing and declaring and believing.

There is a time frame on the word *until*—it means till what you are believing for, anticipating, and expecting actually happens. But for this book, here's the thing about this word *until*—it is never about facts, but faith and truth in God's Word. One thing that you can be absolutely assured of is that your *until* will definitely cost you. It will cost you to a greater degree than you could ever dream possible.

I have learned that there is a wrestling that takes place between your flesh and your faith. The flesh is at all times at enmity with your faith. Faith always denies the flesh, and the flesh always wants to deter and drown out faith. It is a battle between what God has promised and the lies the enemy is trying to make you believe. The lies the enemy spews in your mind tell you that what you're believing for is crazy, absurd, and will never happen. *It is a lie!* But I have discovered in this journey that I can outlast the lies of the enemy and I can last *until* I see victory because of Philippians 4:13:

> *I have strength for all things in Christ Who empowers me [I am ready for anything and equal to anything through Him Who infuses inner strength into me; I am self-sufficient in Christ's sufficiency]* (AMPC).

Every day I was being infused with tenacity, boldness, authority, perseverance, and stamina to not quit! I can honestly say that during that season of my life, I had never experienced anything on that level of intercession in my entire journey in following the Lord, and it cost me in so many ways that I never would have imagined. Jamie and I both went through grueling times in contending for Kaylee's mind, her heart, her spirit, her sanity, and ours too for that matter. I can tell you praying *until* will cost you. Yet I can gladly testify that it has also been one of the greatest joys and undoubtedly the greatest victory of the faithfulness of God and prayer that I have ever encountered.

Isaiah's words explain this in detail concerning our Kaylee and your children as well: *"I and the children the Lord has given me serve as signs"* (Isa. 8:18 NLT).

Today, Kaylee's life is a sign and a wonder to so many people, young and old alike, whom she has touched by her testimony. The anointing on her life carries a genuine heaviness of a glory as she has forged her way through a tumultuous time despite being so young. However, there had to come a time in her life when she realized it was not just going to be her parents' confessions that got her through, but hers as well. In your "pray until" moments, you will come to a realization that yes, *"If two of you shall agree on earth as touching any thing...it shall be done"* (Matt. 18:19), but more than anything, it is going to be *your* made-up mind! *Your* stand and determination! *Your* tenacity to not quit! *Your* declarations of faith!

It may feel as if you are confessing it a thousand times a day, but you can't stop! We did not quit because quitting was not an option, so we pressed on! We pressed on, daring to believe the promises of God in spite of what we saw, thought, or felt. This was the defining moment when our family would never be the same again. Faith will give you the fortitude to pray *until!* However, you have to come to a place in your mind where you count the cost of your *until* and realize that with that cost there will come tests!

Your *Pray Until* Challenge

- After reading this chapter, is there something that comes to your mind to which you need to devote some real-time prayer and fasting *until?*

- Sit down and look at your planner and see when a time of seeking the Lord for a long weekend would be feasible. Don't forget, some things only come through prayer and fasting (see Mark 9:29)!

Note

1.   Hayford, *Prayer Is Invading the Impossible,* 24.

Chapter 2

TESTED FAITH

My fellow believers, when it seems as though you are facing nothing but difficulties, see it as an invaluable opportunity to experience the greatest joy that you can! For you know that when your faith is tested it stirs up in you the power of endurance.

—JAMES 1:2-3 TPT

If there is no strain, there is no strength. ...God does not give us overcoming life; He gives us life as we overcome.

—OSWALD CHAMBERS, *My Utmost for His Highest*

It is not well for a man to pray, cream; and live, skim milk.

—HENRY WARD BEECHER

When you are contending for your *until,* the greatest place you will ever find yourself is where your faith and endurance are being tested. If you live long enough on this planet, you will always find yourself in contention and coming face to face with a *when.* God always speaks louder in the way that you can hear Him the clearest—not in your ears, but through your circumstances.

Peter faced a *when*. Jesus even warned him that it was coming, and he still had to go through it. You see, that is what you do when you come up against a *when*—you go *through it!* Because sometimes God will *not* get you out; He will get you *through!* Jesus said to Peter:

> *Simon, Simon, Satan has asked to sift each of you like wheat. But I have pleaded in prayer for you, Simon, that your faith should not fail. So when you have repented and turned to me again, strengthen your brothers* (Luke 22:31-32 NLT).

I'm so glad that Jesus not only predicted that Peter would go through a *when*, but He also prophesied that he would come out on the other side of his *when*. Jesus knows what you're facing, and this is the Word of the Lord for you:

> *When you pass through the waters, I will be with you; and when you pass through the rivers, they will not sweep over you. When you walk through the fire, you will not be burned; the flames will not set you ablaze* (Isaiah 43:2 NIV).

Paul then says:

> *So now I am glad to boast about my weaknesses, so that the power of Christ can work through me* (2 Corinthians 12:9 NLT).

What you have to understand is that it is not you working; it is the power of Jesus working through you. Watch the enemy at this point, because when you are at your weakest and want to give up the quickest, that is when you will hear the serpent, the devil, speak the loudest, and he will say to you as he said to Eve, "Did God really say...?" (see Gen. 3:1). In other words, "Are you actually going to believe that God can heal you?"

The devil will come to you and say, "Do you know anyone in your family who has ever been healed of this sickness or this disease?" Then the question becomes, "Out of all the people in your family who have suffered with this, can you believe you are the one who is going to be healed of this sickness in Jesus' name?" Always remember, there is an anointing on your life that *attracts attacks* just like when Jesus walked the earth. That is the reason why you look at the trouble you're going through as just a confirmation that you're doing something right.

I love what Chris Blackaby describes as the three realms of faith we can walk in as people of God. When Paul was bit by a serpent on the island of Melita in Acts 28, there were three ways that a Christian walking in faith could look at this particular scenario.

1. The Natural Realm

We can use our faith in the natural realm. Here's what that would look like if it happened to us. We would at once call the paramedics, then start trying to suck the poison out while having faith that the paramedics will arrive on time.

2. The Word of Faith

After the natural realm is the word of faith realm. You get bit by a serpent, and you begin to declare, "In Jesus' name, I shall not die but live to declare the wonderful works of God. No deadly poison shall harm me. No weapon that is formed against me shall be able to prosper" (see Ps. 118:17; Mark 16:18; Isa. 54:17). Basically, you recite all the scriptures on healing, which are all true, and then believe God to honor His Word!

3. *The Supernatural Realm*

The next realm is the realm that Paul walked in, which is the supernatural realm. The Bible says that, *"Paul shook the snake off into the fire and suffered no ill effects"* (Acts 28:5 NIV). In addition, he never mentioned another word about it.

I believe there is a realm we can go to in God where we have so much of God in us, and we believe so fully in the scriptures, that when Paul wrote in Ephesians 2:6 (NIV), *"God raised us up with Christ and seated us with him in the heavenly realms in Christ Jesus,"* he was talking about us.

I believe for a fact that we can be so empowered by God that the things of this earth do not have any power over us. They can't touch us, move us, or diminish us. That's where Jesus lived, and the Bible also says in First John 4:17, *"As he is, so are we in this world."*

I firmly believe the same power that raised Jesus from the dead shall quicken our mortal bodies (see Rom. 8:11). Paul was a witness to the Word that Jesus declared in Luke 10:19:

> *Behold, I give unto you power to tread on serpents and scorpions, and over all the power of the enemy: and nothing shall by any means hurt you.*

So we need to keep growing in His power and consecration and drawing in to Him. When we do, He promises that *"He is a rewarder of those who diligently seek Him*" (Heb. 11:6 NKJV). It is not a casual acquaintance, but it is someone who is after Him and His presence and power in their lives. I love the fact that the Bible says in Luke 4:29-30:

> *They got up and drove him out of the city, and led him to the brow of the hill on which their city had been built, in order to throw him down the cliff. But passing through their midst, he went his way* (NIV).

I would even add *unscathed*. Jesus was in a supernatural realm and the devil couldn't touch Him because it wasn't His time. Wouldn't you love to live in this place at all times? Peter said to Jesus on the Mount of Transfiguration:

> *Lord, it's wonderful for us to be here! If you want, I'll make three shelters as memorials—one for you, one for Moses, and one for Elijah* (Matthew 17:4 NLT).

Jesus told them in essence, "No! We have to go back down from this mountain. There are people who are still in the demon-possessed valley who need us." We can't stay in our prayer chambers and closets all the time. We can't live our lives skipping from church to church or from conference to conference being fed until we are weebles walking around all the time wobbling in revelation. Jesus gave us a commission to go into all the world and make disciples. Let us go where the masses are and preach Jesus and Him crucified.

It is true we go from faith to faith, strength to strength, and from glory to glory. I want all that God has for me, but it will definitely come at a cost.

What we can't do is put our attention on worrying about something that we can't change in our own power. That is not who we are as children of God. Worry won't change anything. If it would, then let's dedicate the next month to just constantly worrying and then believe all of our problems will be solved. That is not how it works.

Jesus said, "Do not fret." Why? Because it leads to trouble. What does that trouble look like? Heart attacks, high blood pressure, emotional issues, especially not building a relationship with the Lord Jesus, and the list goes on.

Look what Job said: *"For the thing I greatly feared has come upon me, and what I dreaded has happened to me"* (Job 3:25 NKJV). Wow! What an incitement against our brother Job. The oldest book in the Bible, yet it is speaking so clearly to us today.

> *Death and life are in the power of the tongue: and they that love it shall eat the fruit thereof* (Proverbs 18:21).

The New Living Translation says, *"Those who love to talk will reap the consequences."* If you talk too much, and if you're not talking faith talk, you will eat everything that your mouth is producing. So be careful with your words when pursuing your *until*, because you may have to eat them later on!

I love that the apostle James gives us a heads-up right here and cautions us, *"when* your faith is tested." As long as you are on planet Earth, there is always an opportunity for your faith to be tested as a believer. Yes, that's right—I did say an opportunity. James says:

> *Consider it pure joy, my brothers and sisters, whenever you face trials of many kinds, because you know that the*

testing of your faith produces perseverance. Let perseverance finish its work so that you may be mature and complete, not lacking anything (James 1:2-4 NIV).

Jesus was tested, the apostles were tested, some of the godliest people we know have been tested, which leads me to believe that I will surely be tested. Peter explains why testing comes, because *"the Spirit of glory and of God rests on you"* (1 Pet. 4:14 NIV).

This scripture is relating to the fact that you are His. By receiving testing with joy, it's the same joy that Jesus expressed, because the scriptures say:

Let us run with perseverance the race marked out for us, fixing our eyes on Jesus, the pioneer and perfecter of faith. For the joy set before him he endured the cross (Hebrews 12:1-2 NIV).

Have you ever noticed someone who was going through a complicated and challenging time in their lives, yet it seemed there was a glory that rested on them? You probably couldn't put your finger on it, but you knew that you knew God was with them. What was it? It was that joy! The same joy that Jesus had when He knew He was a blessing to His Father. That joy was you and me. We are here to be a blessing to our heavenly Father and to bring Him joy and glory.

Also, it gives you faith and tenacity to boldly declare, "I am going to pass this test because I know all the other saints of God who have already gone before me passed tests and trials, and because they passed them they are the great cloud of witnesses who are cheering me on, and I will pass this test as well."

Going through the test of fasting for Kaylee was seriously one of the biggest emotional roller coaster rides I have ever ridden. I would leave for a weekend on a five-day trip, and I would see so many miracles, deliverances, and people being set free from the very thing my daughter was bound by, and yet I would come home to learn that absolutely nothing had changed. The test was merciless!

Strangely, one of the things that would bring me comfort was the fact that I had seen this scenario played out before with my mom and others I had observed growing up. You can always fall back on things you have witnessed with your own eyes and experienced yourself. As the baby out of 12, I had a bird's-eye view of watching my mama pass tests. I was the one who was always around her. I saw the tears; I heard the moaning and the groaning in the spirit realm in her prayer closet (literally) and also outside, as she would hang clothes on the clothes wire. I heard her declaring, "Before I die, I will see all my children come to You, Jesus, but even if I don't, I believe they will still be saved, and I will see them on that great reunion day." She stood on a promise from God in His Word:

> *Believe on the Lord Jesus Christ, and you will be saved, you and your household* (Acts 16:31 NKJV).

My mama knew that all you needed was a promise and a word from God!

Consider this! It's in the runner's last lap that he is tempted to give up and quit! It's when a baseball team is in the ninth inning, two outs, and strike two that they decide, "You know what, this is for the championship and we're going to win this!" Or better yet, there are three seconds to go, the ball is in your hands, and you are at mid-court—can you beat the buzzer and make the shot? Yes, of course you can!

What are those things? Well, it could be called a lot of things. It could be endurance, faith, courage, and determination to get up and pray, be the one to forgive offenses aligned against you, and decide you will be the one to live in victory regardless of what it looks like.

Let this be the day that you begin a fast of seeking the Lord, praying for someone else's children, your neighbor's husband, or for revival in your church and community. I believe when you make up your mind that you will pass the test, there will come a resolve in your heart, spirit, and the deepest part of your soul that says, "I'm going to win this! I'm going to pass this test! I'm going to the other side! I'm coming out! I'm coming in! I'm going over! I'm going to believe—until! I will pass this faith test!"

I remember in the early days when we were believing for doors to open in the ministry and for us to go to the nations, we would pray all night long. Our caregiver would stay with the girls at our house and we would pray from 6:00 p.m. till 6:00 a.m. the next day. Although it was very tiring and would take a lot of energy and stamina, we would do it every month. I really looked forward to those times because they were uninterrupted times of prayer and fasting and communion.

When we look back now, our ministry was marked by those times, our marriage was marked as a couple, and God proved Himself to be so real during those intimate moments. Also, it was during those times when some of the biggest doors were opened to us, and still to this day we enjoy the fruit of them.

I believe God is raising you up to be a strong, resilient, rooted and grounded believer who will not budge in the face of opposition and who is unmovable in times of testing. When you are unmovable in your faith, the enemy is already defeated! However, it is "not by might or by power but by His Spirit" through our child-like trust in Him (see Zech. 4:6). For instance, when the disciples wanted to know what the Kingdom of God really looked like, Jesus sat a child in their midst (see Matt. 18:1-3). God is looking for some children of His—not to be childish, but to be childlike in their faith. A child will believe anything that their father says. Why? Because they have a history with their dad; they know that if their dad makes a promise, he will surely keep it! "How much more!" The Bible says about your heavenly Father:

> *If you then, being evil, know how to give good gifts to your children, how much more will your heavenly Father give...* (Luke 11:13 NKJV).

Oftentimes, the only way to accomplish your *until* moment is through your faith being tested. Of course, the early church knew, and even today the persecuted church knows, what it means to go through a time of a *testing of your faith.* I love that Paul and Barnabas (the encourager) admonished them to:

> *...continue in the faith in spite of all the persecution, reminding them that they must enter into the Kingdom of God through many tribulations* (Acts 14:22 TLB).

Throughout this time of battling for Kaylee against this spirit of fear, one of the most severe tests was to make sure that I put on the armor of God every day. I knew that just as she was in a battle in her mind, I also was fighting against:

...principalities, against powers, against the rulers of the darkness of this world, against spiritual wickedness in high places (Ephesians 6:12).

Just as bad as the devil wanted her, he wanted me as well. As a matter of fact, he wanted both of us and my and Jamie's marriage. Only God and the married couple knows the strain that something of this magnitude puts on a marriage. Believe me when I tell you, if you don't already know, the enemy is always after your seed. He knows where to hit you, and it is always below the belt. He knows somebody is always waiting for us on the other side, so he wants to stop that. The great news is, there is so much victory and joy on the other side of your obedience. Someone is waiting for you to finish your *until* moment so you can help them get through theirs.

What did it look like on a day-to-day basis to fight for our *until*? Jamie and I were constantly reminding Kaylee of what the Word says about her. Also, we listened to wisdom from godly counselors, friends, and Kingdom people. We also kept her engaged in doing things that she needed to do to keep her mind occupied. It meant making her get up out of bed and helping her make her bed when she couldn't do it on her own. It meant making sure that she was bathing properly, brushing her teeth, getting dressed by herself, going downstairs, and eating something, even if it was a few crackers. It meant many tears at first, and constantly encouraging her to *change her mind*. It meant keeping her in the house of God, even if it meant her holding on to me for dear life.

We had to also maintain our relationship with Erica and keep interaction going between both of them and strive to keep things as normal as possible. So what we could do in the natural, we did it, and what we could encourage and decree and declare in the supernatural, we did that as well. Obviously, there was more warfare in the supernatural than the natural. We wanted God to get the glory at the end *when* He delivered Kaylee. We knew that God was giving us wisdom and understanding as we constantly prayed for it, but we also knew faith without works is dead (see James 2:17).

Here's what we found out. When God asks you to do something possible and you do it, God will honor that if you're using the common sense He gave you. But God will also ask you to do something impossible, crazy, and foolish to the world's eyes, and He will honor that as well, even if no one else is watching, and He will get *all* the glory for it.

I remember very specifically one day after Jamie had dropped Kaylee off at school. The night before had been very challenging, and no one had gotten any sleep—especially Kaylee. After Jamie had dropped her off at school, we found ourselves upstairs in her room as we often did, praying, declaring, repenting of anything we could possibly think of that, just by chance, could be hindering our prayers. I was so shocked to see my husband, as he was sobbing, all of a sudden begin to get between the box spring and the mattress of her bed. You have to envision him crawling in between her box spring and her mattress, weeping and crying out to God in desperation. As I watched him I thought to myself, *This is extreme, what is he doing?* "Babe," I said, "What are you doing? Why are you doing that?"

He said, very nonchalantly, "This is a place in her room where we haven't prayed yet."

You may ask, what happened after what seemed like such a very dramatic instruction? I can honestly say nothing, in the natural, but in the supernatural the grip of hell's paws got a little looser. One instruction from God, no matter how absurd, can destroy many chains in our lives. So, when going after your *until* moment, anytime God challenges you to do the seemingly crazy and impossible thing, it's not so you will get the glory. It will be so people will say, "God used that! God did that!"

What I learned is that a crisis always reveals a person's true character. In those hard times, there was never a question of, "Do I have time to pray today? Do I have time to be in the Word today?" No! That was my bread and living water. Here's another thing that I was grateful for—I'm glad I didn't have to wait to get God's attention. God and I had already been talking and communicating; we were very much acquainted with each other, because:

> He walks with me, and He talks with me
>
> And He tells me I am His own
>
> And the joy we share as we tarry there
>
> None other has ever known![1]

Why? Because the battleground is in your prayer closet, in the car, on your knees beside your bed, in the wee hours of the morning, or maybe between a box spring and a mattress. It will not happen when you say, "Wow, this is a hard time in my life right now, I guess I'd better pray about it." No! That is not the time to build a relationship with God that is unshakable. You have to be ready with weapons in hand at all times. When you are on a battleground and you are not prepared with your weapons, you will be destroyed along with everything that is precious to you.

Remember Nehemiah? When being threatened by Sanballat and Tobiah, he admonished the exiles to *"work with one hand supporting their load and one hand holding a weapon"* (Neh. 4:17 NLT). Never forget, even Jesus warned us that the thief comes to steal, kill, and destroy (see John 10:10), so be vigilant!

Oftentimes in your *until* moments, the Holy Spirit will take you through a different way than what you anticipated and a different understanding of what He really wants for you and the situation you are believing God for. Whether you believe it or not, God has bigger things in mind than just your *until* moment. He had to get you to this place to get you to the next. What is the next? Well, let's see!

Your *Pray Until* Challenge

- Is there something strange and radical that you feel you are supposed to do in obedience to an action or instruction? Do it and believe God!

- Is God speaking to you about a particular room in your home, your business, or anywhere else that would seem a radical instruction to pray an unusual prayer?

Note

1. C. Austin Miles, "I Come to the Garden Alone," 1913, public domain.

Chapter 3

CEASELESS PRAYER: THE SECRET REVEALED

Be joyful in hope, patient in affliction, faithful in prayer.
—ROMANS 12:12 NIV

Character cannot be developed in ease and quiet. Only through experience of trial and suffering can the soul be strengthened, vision cleared, ambition inspired, and success achieved.

—HELEN KELLER

Prayer should be the key of the day, and the lock of the night.

—OWEN FELTHAM,
Resolves, Divine, Moral and Political

I don't know if you know what I'm talking about or have lived long enough to be around what I like to call "the old folk." In other words, the first- and second-row saints, the intercessors, the amen corner, the fire-starters, the huddle, whatever you want to call them. They were the elite group, the rare, the extraordinary, the called out, the mothers in Israel, the church mamas and fathers.

Oh no, they didn't play! They were serious about their God, their church, and their prayer life. They were convinced of the old Gospel hymn, "Just a little talk with Jesus makes it right."

I love what E.M. Bounds said: "The Church is looking for better methods; God is looking for better men" (and women!). When we stand before the Lord, we will not hear, "Well done, My good and faithful pastor, bishop, evangelist, apostle, preacher, missionary, teacher, singer, or worship leader." We will hear, "Well done, My good and faithful *servant.*"

Those church mothers and fathers had a relationship with God that made all of hell tremble. Now don't get me wrong—they didn't claim to be all that. When I was growing up in my church, this wasn't a title or a special position that was awarded them. They were just humble servants of God. They didn't brag about it; they didn't put their sweaters down and save their seats so nobody else would get their place—no, they were there because they had paid a price and they were involuntarily appointed by God. And believe me when I tell you, nobody wanted their seat because of the price that was paid for them to be able to sit in those seats.

My sister and I would observe them, our eyes glued to what was happening in the service. It was anyone's guess what would happen next. We didn't know if the Spirit would break out, if there would be a message given out in tongues that would make the very hairs on your body stand up, if someone would collapse in the spirit "under the power," or if there would be a "Jericho march." Our little eyes were glued to "said person in the spirit, on the floor, seemingly not breathing." Then, if someone gave out a message in tongues, who would be the one to interpret it? What would be said?

Growing up as we did on those pews, we never knew what would happen. Sinners might be moved to run to an altar, someone would receive their healing and deliverance, or it might just turn into an old-fashioned testimony service. Whatever it was that happened, I can tell you there were some wide-eyed children who were watching, and it forever marked us all.

One thing that all of these saints of God had in common was that they all had the same spiritual DNA when it came to the things of God. So it wasn't strange to see them together. It didn't matter where they found themselves—on the front row or in the altar praying—you knew when Sister Carolina, Sister Toomoney, Sister Della Jane, and my Aunt Mary Lee started jerking in the Holy Ghost, it was more than likely going to be a chain reaction. When that happened, it wouldn't be long before the whole row would be jerking, dancing, shouting, hairpins flying everywhere, hair falling down from their ever-so-gingerly put together Pentecostal buns. It could be one or two, or it could be all five, or the whole two or three rows, which ended up being 12 to 15 of them at the same time, and I can tell you, *it was real*.

They were always together, whether it was homecoming with "dinner on the ground," going to each other's houses to pray, and sitting together at camp meetings or prayer conferences. But especially at their assignment on those church pews, as the service would begin and throughout the entire church service, there was ceaseless prayer going on—mainly praying in the Holy Ghost.

Growing up watching this phenomenon take place, I didn't know at the time just exactly what it was and what was going on, but I certainly know now. I would give anything to be able to go back and experience those times again. They prayed and spoke in tongues seemingly all the time. They fasted together corporately, separately, knowing, and unknowing. There was such a camaraderie with each other that nothing really had to be said; they just knew their lane and they stayed in it. When they talked on the phone it was just like being in church with them. They were praying, talking in tongues, laughing, sharing testimonies, and just experiencing love, joy, and peace in the Holy Ghost. Don't get me wrong, they had their share of tests and trials and difficulties, but they had learned the secret—*ceaseless prayer.* That generation knew how to pray! That was their wheelhouse and they were very well acquainted with the One to whom they prayed.

As I am writing these words, I want to encourage you to have the kind of faith that operates in a ceaseless prayer. You may not have lived during those very special times, or maybe you did, but you still need a revival in your soul. Perhaps you have experienced some coolness in your spirit that needs to be rekindled so that you will burn like fire as the saints of yesteryear used to burn with. One thing I know for sure—God hears desperate prayers from the hearts of desperate people.

We are to pray loud prayers, audacious prayers, fearless prayers, and the God-kind of prayers. Prayer in its simplest form is communication with our Creator. Prayer is our assignment as a believer. Prayer is the avenue to get to our moment of miracle because anything spiritual is built by prayer.

Jesus taught that men ought always to pray and not to faint (see Luke 18:1). Jesus very emphatically said *when* you pray, *when* you fast, and *when* you give. There is an expectation for every believer to do what Jesus instructed us to do. The psalmist put it this way:

In the morning, Lord, you hear my voice; in the morning I lay my requests before you and wait expectantly (Psalm 5:3 NIV).

I love what Oswald Chambers said in *My Utmost for His Highest*:

We must go to God as His child, because only a child gets his prayers answered; a "wise" man does not (see Matthew 11:25).

Sometimes when we come to God we feel as if we must come with our thees, thuses, and thous, but what I found out in my *until* times is that prayer in its simplest form is just talking to God like you would talk to your best friend. We want to sometimes impress God with our words, postures, and intellect, but the Father just simply wants us to come. The Bible says that God would come down *"in the cool of the day"* to talk to Adam and Eve (Gen. 3:8). What I know about God is that He will come in the cool of the day or in the middle of your hot mess to talk to you. He will meet you right where you are.

Our job and duty is to pray. Just pray! That's all! Very simply put! We labor in *His* vineyard. It is the Lord's vineyard and not ours. Matthew 9:38 says, *"Pray the Lord of the harvest to send out laborers into His harvest"* (NKJV).

Let me give you an example. You probably don't get goosebumps every time you have to go in to your nine-to-five job every day to labor for someone else's vision. However, your employer is the one who thought about the particular job that you are assigned to. It is their creativity that put you in a position to get a job to help make their dream become a reality—thus, your paycheck. In the same way, as children of the Most High God, it is our labor in prayer for the Father's agenda that makes His dreams possible. When we labor in prayer from the Father's perspective, something great always happens. That is the reason He says *when* you pray. It is expected!

Jesus said, *"Men* [and women] *ought always to pray, and not to faint"* (Luke 18:1). Sometimes you don't know how to pray and that is why Jude said, *"Build each other up in your most holy faith, pray in the power of the Holy Spirit"* (Jude 20 NLT).

I think one of the things that we forget is that prayer is conversational. In other words, prayer is a dialogue, not a monologue. So one of the things that I have learned is to be still and quiet before the Lord and listen to what He says.

I can't tell you how often instruction would come as Jamie and I would pray together, separately, or most of the night. During those times, the Spirit of God was always talking, instructing, encouraging, admonishing, and building us up. We prayed with His agenda in mind: "Father, *'Your Kingdom come. Your will be done on earth as it is in heaven'"* (Matt. 6:10 NKJV).

Jesus wants to do for you everything you can imagine so that His Father may receive all glory and honor. Believe me when I tell you, every time I see Kaylee with a microphone in her hand, declaring and worshiping and preaching and prophesying, I know the Father gets more pleasure out of it than I could ever imagine. When I see her throw her head back and begin to laugh, just like her Grandma Jacobs used to laugh with every fiber of her being, the Father gets pleasure from it, and hell boils over with disgust because of it! Hallelujah!

I have many such testimonies in my arsenal of ceaseless prayer for miracles to come forth. One of the strongest testimonies is when my husband, as a college student, led a group overseas on a missions trip to the Philippines. Jamie comes from a very godly family, and we were both raised on the road with our families. At the very young age of five years old, he was playing drums. Jamie's family was very gifted and had a beautiful harmony as a singing group. His mother, Parmalee, was one of those mothers who always covered her children with prayer and love. His father, Don, is a very accomplished pianist and an incredible father and grandfather. They were a family that was and is to this day very close. Growing up in church, they were very much involved and they also had to learn to balance road ministry with school and family life.

As time passed, each child began to find their own way, and Jamie found himself at college studying ministry and pursuing the call of God on his life. At the end of his sophomore year, plans were being made to go on a three-month trip to the Philippines during the summer, which he would be helping to lead.

Every semester at his private college, the student body looked forward to their convocation. When it came time for the spring revival, there was a special speaker who came in to lead by the name of Mark Rutland. Before the revival ended on the last night, the leaders suggested praying for the team going to the Philippines over the summer. One by one, everyone was prayed over, and Jamie was one of the last ones Dr. Rutland prayed and spoke over. As he prayed this ordinary prayer, "God bless him, give him wisdom and direction as he helps to lead this group," all of a sudden he prayed, "and Lord, be with him, especially when he gets separated from the rest of the group, and bring him through."

To Jamie, everything was great and good until Dr. Rutland prayed that prayer, and then it was like, "Okay, what just happened

45

here? What did he mean by *when he gets separated from the rest of the group?* Jamie says, "I remember looking up into Dr. Rutland's face and thinking, *Is this a prophecy, a warning, or just a passing thought?*" As a young Bible student, he just didn't know. It was especially disconcerting, but nevertheless he shrugged it off. His mother, however, didn't! She was kind of like Mary—she pondered these things in her heart. So, she did what any mother does—she began to pray, and to pray ceaselessly, just like she had always done as a young girl growing up in a pastor's home.

The months turned into weeks and the weeks turned into days, and all of a sudden it was time to leave for the much-anticipated missions trip. As the group landed in Manilla at 11 p.m., it was the rainy season. As they began to leave the airport, the roads were flooded, people were walking in knee-deep water, and the threat of mudslides was looming over their heads. Yet it seemed as if this was the common way of life for the Filipinos. For Jamie and the students, it was just exciting to reach the destination of the unknown. Things began to go by speedily with their schedule. Overseas trips are no joke, and they are not for the faint of heart either. You're either very much ready or you're not—it's just that simple. With such a large group, which was a blessing, to cover more ground and territory, many times they would go separate ways and come back together after church for a meal.

The first month into the trip, they were scheduled at a particular church where they all would be ministering together. They had been traveling all day to get to this city for an open-air meeting. They were running behind and were not able to eat the meal that was prepared for them in advance, so they had to go into service without eating. After service, Jamie and the others began to eat the food that had been sitting out for quite some time. He didn't realize it, but his whole life was about to flash before his eyes.

The wee hours of the morning found him and only him in excruciating pain in his abdomen. What followed was someone dropped him off at the closest hospital, which was located in the mountains. However, the team had to keep moving to make the appointments that had been scheduled months in advance. Of course, you guessed it—he got separated from his team.

The fever and dehydration were now taking a toll on his body. Although IVs were pumping him with fluid and he had ice packs on his head, nothing seemed to change. Jamie was mortified by the conditions of the hospital in the early '80s—it was typical of a third-world country with its archaic surroundings and equipment.

Across the way, a woman was undergoing surgery, apparently without anesthesia, with only a thin curtain separating her from other patients, and screams of terror were coming from her. On the other side of him was a man in such pain that all he could do was moan and groan, crying out for help. Jamie's entire body and his emotions were in total shock as he was witnessing these things and progressively getting sicker.

All of a sudden, this female doctor pulled back the curtain and began to explain to him in her broken English what was going on in his body. She began, "Mr. Tuttle, you fully dehydrated, you might not live." She explained, "Your body in lots of shock, we hope to get fluids built up, if not, you die, you very sick!" Can you imagine getting this news 10,000 miles from your family? There were no cell phones, no pagers, no emails—there was only the power of prayer, and that was all that was needed.

Meanwhile, back at home in North Carolina, in the wee hours of the morning Jamie's mom couldn't sleep because she felt that something was wrong with Jamie. So under the unction of the Holy Spirit she got out of bed and began to crawl into the closet on top of her husband's shoes and pray. This was her place of prayer where she often met with the Lord. She believed in the scripture literally when it says:

When thou prayest, enter into thy closet, and when thou hast shut the door, pray to thy Father (Matthew 6:6).

Now, this prayer was not just your ordinary, "I'm going to spend a little time in prayer" prayer. No! This was a desperate, Heaven-shaking quickening in her spirit to touch God for her son, because Jamie was in trouble and something was going on with him. I can tell you that God heard that mama's prayer, because two days later he got up off that deathbed and left that hospital. *Hallelujah!*

The devil tried to kill my future husband and the girls' future dad, but ceaseless prayer was being offered up, not only by his mom but also by other intercessors all over the world whom God had awakened to pray for His servant. After three days in the hospital and a ten-day separated journey to recovery, God raised Jamie up, and he celebrated the fulfillment of Dr. Rutland's words that said, "You will come through." He was able to finish out the assignment with lives being changed in ways he never would have believed or thought.

Think of the concept of prayer as breath in your lungs and blood from your heart. The blood flows and the breath in our lungs continues without ceasing. We don't even think about it, but the fact of the matter is, it never stops. In the same way we should let prayer be a ceaseless flowing from one moment to the next.

The outcome for my husband could have been quite different if not for *"the effectual fervent prayer"* of a mom who knew when to pray and how to pray. The secret is to know that whenever you call, He hears and answers your prayers because there is an ongoing conversation that can always be interrupted with a, *"Dear Father, I need a miracle right now,"* and He responds! But we have to learn the secret of being a "diligent seeker." There is a place you go in prayer, there is a position you take in prayer, and there is definitely a posture you take in prayer. Let's see what that looks like!

Your *Pray Until* Challenge

- Have you ever felt like you were thrown into a mode of ceaseless prayer? What did it look like? What were the results?

- When was the last time you felt childlike when you prayed? Do it again, or for the first time.

- Surround yourself often with some old folk. Listen to and learn from them.

- Do you remember your first love? Ask Jesus to rekindle the Holy Spirit fire once again as in yesteryears. Tell Him to take you back to your first love!

Chapter 4

THE POSTURE OF UNTIL

So Ahab went up to eat and drink. And Elijah went up to the top of Carmel; then he bowed down on the ground, and put his face between his knees.

—1 KINGS 18:42 NKJV

It is not a matter of time so much as a matter of heart; if you have the heart to pray, you will find the time.

—CHARLES SPURGEON, *"Peter's Shortest Prayer"*

To get nations back on their feet, we must first get down on our knees.

—BILLY GRAHAM

It had been a long and arduous day for Jesus. The whole reason He came into this earth was getting ready to be fulfilled to the letter, and Jesus even said, *"My time is at hand"* (Matt. 26:18). I can only imagine the utter disappointment of the disciples hearing, *"One of you shall betray me"* (Matt. 26:21). The Bible goes on to say that they were *"exceeding sorrowful"* when they heard this (Matt. 26:22). It was at this time that Jesus began to share with them the bread and the wine. Lots of emotions and revelations were getting

51

ready to unfold. The bewilderment, confusion, and perplexity of this moment was numbing, considering that everything over the past three and a half years was on the line in a matter of minutes. But look at Jesus—look at His posture in this most defining moment of His entire life as Son of Man. He had washed and wiped the disciples' feet, encouraged them, shared with them the most intimate communion, and then He was overwhelmed with sorrow Himself.

Then came the walk to the Garden of Gethsemane, with literally the weight of the world on His shoulders. He invited His closest companions to come and go with Him—Peter, James, and John. He said to them, *"My soul is overwhelmed with sorrow to the point of death. Stay here and keep watch with me"* (Matt. 26:38 NIV).

Jesus was saying, in essence, "I want you to take on the posture of watching with Me." In other words, He was saying to those sleepy disciples, "Come and go with Me so I won't be by Myself. Stay here by My side, don't leave Me, I need you," and He even went as far as to say, *"Watch and pray, that ye enter not into temptation"* (Matt. 26:41). He was pouring His whole heart out to the three men who knew Him more than any of the others, and in essence He exclaimed, "I'm in great agony of spirit. I need you to stand with Me, sit with Me, pray with Me, but whatever you do, don't go to sleep on Me, but keep your faith active with Me."

You see, there is a posture in prayer that must be taken on when you are praying for a breakthrough. It is an unashamedly violent posture of determination in your heart, mind, and spirit that things will change. Your prayer posture can come in varied and different situations—sometimes at the most inopportune times, or so you think. When you are in a posture of *until prayer,* you refuse to stray from your position because you are sold out to the idea that you're committed and you refuse to be refused!

It reminds me of when a 747 is on the runway preparing for takeoff, the pilot signals to the tower that he needs permission to take off into flight. The tower will then either give him permission, hold him steady, or delay altogether. Once the tower has secured all things, the flight is ready for takeoff. The tower will then give him the signal, "You are allowed to take the runway." Once on the runway, there is only a certain amount of time allotted before another airline or plane will be either landing or taking off, so the idea is to get up as soon as possible. Once the pilot takes off down the runway, there has to be a clear message that goes to the tower that says, "We are committed." That means no stopping, no slowing down, no turning back—they are either going up, or something else, but that particular plane is committed to go! That's what it looks like to say, "My posture will not change, I have a made-up mind, I'm going to see a victory for the battle belongs to the Lord."

As a matter of fact, I remember on one particular occasion I was up in the air 30 thousand feet, I had my headphones on listening to worship music, and quite honestly I was oblivious to what was happening around me. Jamie was sitting next to me, busy passing the time away watching some sports. This was at a very crucial time with Kaylee, and we were in faith and confessing and believing that at any minute we would get a phone call, a message, or something that said, "Things have turned around and Kaylee is free." Faith, along with expectation, was our lifeline that kept us motivated.

As the music was playing in my ears, all of a sudden I felt the sweet presence of God come into that first-class cabin. I thought to myself, *Oh, how I wish I were home instead of on this plane. I would just love to pour out my heart to God in worship right now!* Then the tears began to drop uncontrollably. I thought to myself, *Uh oh! What am I going to do?*

Well, one thing I am particular about is not leaving home without a coat for my body and a scarf for my neck. Whether it is summer or winter, I always have one with me. It doesn't have to be a heavy one, but one that will keep the rain off and give me a little warmth on a sometimes chilly plane. So as I glanced down at my coat on my legs I thought, *Why not!* I took that coat and pulled it over my head, and suddenly I felt like I was in the Holy of Holies. The worship was resounding in my ears, I had on my ugly-cry face, and the sweetness of Jesus filled my heart. Oh no, it wasn't a prayer shawl; I wasn't in a grandiose, spectacular cathedral; I wasn't screaming and hollering and scaring people—it was just me, my worship music, and a coat.

The posture of prayer is not so much in the details but in the determination to get in a position to receive what He has for us right then and there. I had postured myself to receive what the Holy Spirit wanted to do in my life at that moment, and it was glorious! I can tell you when I walked off that plane, I was much lighter than before I got on it. I had the victory!

Here's the point of the matter—we are always watching for Jesus. We are waiting to see when He is going to do what He said He would do. We find ourselves watching to see if today will be the day. Who is He going to use? What will it look like? We just know He is the miracle worker and at any given moment something is getting ready to change. It is a spirit of expectancy! This moment is like the woman with the issue of blood:

For she kept saying to herself, "If I could touch even his clothes, I know I will be healed" (Mark 5:28 TPT).

Her posture was, "It doesn't matter if I have to crawl to get to Jesus, if I get stepped on, or pushed to the side—I've just got to get to where He is. He is passing by here in my village, and this is my opportunity to get what I have been dreaming about and I will not miss my moment." And she didn't!

Nobody wants to go to Gethsemane, nobody wants to go to the pressing place, including Jesus. He wanted to obey His Father, but because He was omnipotent (all-knowing), He knew what He would have to go through. But look at His posture—Jesus found a place in prayer that brought the angels of God to come to His side and minister to Him and bring comfort.

What is on the other side of your posture of staying and tarrying? In this posture of Gethsemane that you may be in right now, you may be tired, feel like all is lost, hopelessness has settled in, and you are feeling alone. Maybe you *are* alone, but you can't give in to your feelings, not now—you're almost there!

Jesus is trying to bring something out of you through this trial, situation, hurt, and pain. You can't see the reason for the *extreme posture* that He is inviting you to take part in, but you have to understand—*sometimes in order to have what you have never had before, you have to do something you have never done before*. It all goes back to the cost of following Jesus, of seeing deliverance, of seeing victory, of seeing purpose fulfilled in your prodigal's life or your marriage.

There was a time in Kaylee's life of battling this fear when we looked this young girl in those beautiful hazel eyes and told her,

"Kaylee, now it's your turn! Dad and I can't do this *for* you any-more; we need you to come alongside of us and grab hold of your Gethsemane. We want you to know we will continue to watch with you, and be assured, we will not go to sleep on you, but now there's something that you have to do, honey—you've got to contend for your own deliverance." That was a very painful time in all of our lives. We gave her the tools, we taught her how to use the weap-ons that we gave her—now it was time for her to engage with her enemy eyeball to eyeball. She had to rise to the occasion. She had to get in a prayer posture and in a position she had never been in before and face her Goliath and her Red Sea.

Your *pray until* is bigger than a mom and dad; it's bigger than your church intercessors, your posse. Now it becomes personal—*you* need to press. Kaylee started quoting the scriptures that I gave her time and time again; she started having her own communion, spending countless hours in her room worshiping and drawing into the presence of God.

I remember that Erica would come to Jamie and me, with her little analytical self, and say something like, "Mom she has been in her room for four hours. Don't you think it's time she came out of that room to be with the rest of us?"

We would tell Erica, "No, Erica, she is okay; she and Jesus are working everything out."

At the time, they shared something of a suite together—they had separate rooms, but only a double door separated them from each other. So the music, worship, and praise coming from Kaylee's room was very much heard and seen by Erica. "But Mom," she would say, "I need to do my homework and that music is too loud."

We would tell her, "Well then, go in my and dad's room and use my space." She would hurriedly collect her stuff and go skipping into our room. Looking back, that was probably where she wanted the conversation to go.

Before it was all over with, Kaylee had so influenced Erica in seeking after God that she would join in with her, and they began to worship and sing together. Now, years later, out of all of that has come K+E (Kaylee + Erica) with both of them ministering at youth conferences, churches, and different venues using their gifts and anointings. It all happened because Kaylee got herself in a posture of learning, "This is how I fight my battles!"

It matters how you approach God in this season of your life! It matters that you go the extra mile! It matters that you take a chunk out of your week to fast and pray! It matters that you heed the voice of God in obedience and do whatever He tells you to do, regardless of how foolish it may sound, feel, or even be. Just do it, because on the other side of faith and obedience there is a breakthrough!

I have found out that obedience ignites faith in you. At first, you may not even recognize it, but there is something in you that rises up the very moment you do what God tells you to do. It feels like you can take on the world. As David said, *"For by You I can run against a troop, by my God I can leap over a wall"* (Ps. 18:29 NKJV).

It really brings the super into your natural and you find yourself operating and declaring faith and confidence. Faith is not useless, neither is it incapable of producing seed, but it is very demonstrative. Faith demonstrates itself. It is not founded on how you feel, what you see, or what your mind tells you. The essence of faith is simply to believe the unbelievable! Then watch how God will honor that faith in Him!

I love the way that the Bible describes Noah's posture in walking by faith. It was a walk of obedience, and when you see Noah in Genesis 6, you see faith at work. The Bible begins to describe the posture of this man called Noah.

> *Noah was a righteous man, the only blameless person living on earth at the time, and he walked in close fellowship with God* (Genesis 6:9 NLT).

God found in Noah a man whom He could trust to be obedient in all that was told to him. He walked in high integrity and he was a man who feared God. When you think about it, Enoch and Noah had a lot in common because they were both men of God who had reputations that they "walked with God."

I believe that God wants us to be in alignment with Him, and it involves more than just a Sunday morning stroll; He wants fellowship with us all week long. The Bible says that Noah walked with God, and he was on the same page with God. Although he was not perfect, he made his decision based on having a great desire to be pleasing to the Lord.

It definitely was not easy for Noah to walk with God in the culture that he was living in. The world around him was very similar to the days we find ourselves living in now. The Bible says:

> *Now God saw that the earth had become corrupt and was filled with violence. God observed all this corruption in the world, for everyone on earth was corrupt* (Genesis 6:11-12 NLT).

What a statement that the Bible uses: *"everyone on earth was corrupt."* Everyone! That's a lot of people! But the Bible goes on to say that, *"Noah found grace in the eyes of the Lord"* (Gen. 6:8 NKJV).

There was enough grace to get Noah, his wife, his three sons, and their wives to the other side of the flood and literally start the world all over again, because they found out God's grace was everything that He said it would be. The grace of God will get you to the other side of your flood like Noah, your lion's den like Daniel, and your driest season like Elijah.

Elijah had an *until* moment praying for rain. First of all, James defines who Elijah was:

> *Elijah was a man with a nature like ours, and he prayed earnestly that it would not rain: and it did not rain on the land for three years and six months* (James 5:17 NKJV).

Oh boy, is that encouraging! Elijah was a man *just like us.* Sometimes we look at the people in the Bible and think that they had special superpowers like some Marvel character, but I love how very practical the Bible is. The Bible says that Elijah was just like us with similar passions, yet he prayed and God heard that prayer and many more prayers that Elijah prayed. It is especially interesting the posture that we observe in the prophet. In his place of faith, what he prophesied came to pass for exactly how long he said— three and one-half years.

Now comes the next challenge—it's time for the rain to come again. Faith always keeps you on your toes and your knees. There are always new levels of faith and prayer, always! Elijah presents Ahab with a challenge to see who the real God is, so he says:

> *"Now bring two bulls. The prophets of Baal may choose whichever one they wish and cut it into pieces and lay it*

on the wood of their altar, but without setting fire to it. I will prepare the other bull and lay it on the wood on the altar, but not set fire to it. Then call on the name of your god, and I will call on the name of the Lord. The god who answers by setting fire to the wood is the true God!" And all the people agreed (1 Kings 18:23-24 NLT).

Well, we all know how they did everything they could think of until time for the evening sacrifice, and then Elijah said, "Now it's my turn!" and of course the fire fell and licked up all the water and the sacrifice.

Elijah finished the showdown on Mount Carmel with all the prophets of Baal and proved that the God who answered by fire was and is the one true and living Jehovah God. Elijah then said to the people:

Take the prophets of Baal; let not one of them escape. And they took them: and Elijah brought them down to the brook Kishon, and slew them there (1 Kings 18:40).

Well, this sent shockwaves across the kingdom. Jezebel found out that Elijah had killed all of her prophets and sent word through a messenger to Elijah:

May the gods strike me and even kill me if by this time tomorrow I have not killed you just as you killed them (1 Kings 19:2 NLT).

The Bible says that Elijah once again prophesied to Ahab, and now instead of saying there would be no rain, he said, *"Go up, eat and drink; for there is the sound of abundance of rain"* (1 Kings 18:41 NKJV).

Look at the progression of his posture: first he bowed down on the ground, which speaks of *humility and submission* (see 1 Kings 18:42). Then he began to pray and petition the Lord, and watch what came next. Look at his posture: he *"put his face between his knees,"* which represented *focused faith.* This posture may seem so radical to you as you read this, but in those days, it was *the birthing posture.* Elijah was so focused on seeing the *until* that it meant getting in a position that was totally awkward and probably painful, intense, and strange-looking, but he was desperate for rain. Then look at the perseverance of Elijah:

[Elijah] *said to his servant, "Go up now, look toward the sea." So he went up and looked, and said, "There is nothing"* (1 Kings 18:43 NKJV).

Let me ask you a question, "How desperate are you?" Are you in a place where it seems you have planted seed and yet there is no fruit to this dry season you find yourself in? But look at the tenacity of Elijah—he commanded the servant to go look again and then again and again.

And seven times he said, "Go again." Then it came to pass the seventh time, that he said, "There is a cloud, as small as a man's hand, rising out of the sea!" (1 Kings 18:43-44 NKJV)

Oh yes, now that is *pray until* faith!

Here is what I know about faith—*it always sees.* When you see faith, you have to declare faith. Elijah said to his servant, *"Go up, say to Ahab, 'Prepare your chariot, and go down before the rain stops you'"* (1 Kings 18:44 NKJV). He was saying, "You had better get ready, Ahab, it's going to rain, it's going to rain!" The Bible says:

Now it happened in the meantime that the sky became black with clouds and wind, and there was a heavy rain (1 Kings 18:45 NKJV).

This next part is just like our God:

Then the hand of the Lord came upon Elijah; and he girded up his loins and ran ahead of Ahab to the entrance of Jezreel (1 Kings 18:46 NKJV).

That is the victory of prayer—to outrun your enemies. I believe that God is placing you in a position to see the destruction of your enemies. Observe Moses' *until* moment. God told Moses to tell the children of Israel:

Don't be afraid. Just stand still and watch the Lord rescue you today. The Egyptians you see today will never be seen again (Exodus 14:13 NLT).

I believe that is a word of the Lord for somebody who is reading this right now! God is about to put you in a position that you will literally outrun the devil and overrun every enemy of your life, and you will see a victory you never even imagined before. Moses told the people, "The enemy you are seeing today, you will never see them again!"

When we were in the fight for our lives with Kaylee, the posture I found myself in was a posture I had observed my mama use. It was a posture I had seen people in my church use, and I saw the results. Prayer works! Faith works! And the way you approach a situation in your life matters!

I believe you are one "hallelujah" away from your *until* miracle. You are one fast away from victory! You are one Jericho march away from deliverance. Come on! Let's get going; there are some *big* things ahead of you!

Your *Pray Until* Challenge

This week in your prayer time, do something different in your time with God and His Word, such as:

- Walk when you pray
- Clap your hands when you make a declaration
- You may even want to spend some time lying prostrate on the floor
- Could it be that you are so desperate that you would put your face between your knees as Elijah did? Or something similar?

Chapter 5

Pray Big Until Prayers

*Call unto me, and I will answer thee and show thee great
and mighty things, which thou knowest not.*
—Jeremiah 33:3

The secret of success in Christ's Kingdom is the ability
to pray.
—E.M. Bounds, *Purpose in Prayer*

I have found that there are three stages in every great
work of God: first, it is impossible, then it is difficult,
then it is done.
—Hudson Taylor (1832-1905),
British Christian Missionary to China[1]

Jesus *always* answers prayer. There is no mention in the Bible
of Jesus *not* answering prayer. There *are* some instances where
it mentions people who had small faith, maybe, but Matthew says
everyone who asks receives (see Matt. 7:8)!

I love what my husband says: "It's our responsibility to ask
God. It's God's responsibility to respond to our asking." He may
not answer our prayers exactly how we anticipate that He will, or

even how we want Him to, but He always answers prayer. It may be "yes" or "no" or "it's not time yet" or "I'm going to do it this way," but He answers in the best way every single time! And here's the reason why—He is God and we are not!

There are many things I have learned about my heavenly Father, and one thing I know about God is, God is not stingy. He always gives from His abundance. Not our abundance! So don't expect a natural blessing from Him—His blessings are always supernatural. You have to understand that God blesses two things—*faith and obedience.* In this chapter, I want to encourage you that when you pray *until* prayers, make sure they are *big until prayers!* Here's why, my friend—anything is possible with God (see Matt. 19:26).

Someone has said, "Jesus is the answer, now what was the question?" The Bible says that our days are numbered on this big blue planet. The psalmist speaks of our days like this:

> *Our days may come to seventy years, or eighty, if our strength endures; yet the best of them are but trouble and sorrow, for they quickly pass, and we fly away* (Psalm 90:10 NIV).

So there may be 70 or 80 years, but I want those years to count if there are 40 more left or if there are a 100 of them left. I want it all to count for the glory of God the Father.

There are many testimonies in my and Jamie's life together where we have prayed big prayers and we have seen God answer those big prayers with big answers. A prime example is how we were in need of office space after the CD "There Is No God Like Jehovah" was released. It was really exciting when it hit the streets, as they say, and at the time we were renting a loft office downtown.

The office was really quaint and sweet but there was one problem—the roof leaked. Every time it rained, which was often in the Tennessee Valley, we had to put out buckets all over the floor. That was not our favorite thing to do, but we had no choice; it was the only office space that we felt we could afford.

We had one computer for the office at the time, and we were all just beginning to learn about computers. I don't think either Jamie or I will ever forget coming in from a weekend trip, having been gone from a Wednesday through Sunday, and walking in our office on a Monday morning only to discover there was water everywhere. You guessed it—the computer was drenched with water and was completely dead. It had crashed and it was gone.

To say that we were discouraged and aggravated at the same time was an understatement. It was at that moment the proverbial straw broke the camel's back for my husband. He was fed up, and he was telling God how fed up he was about all of it. One thing we had to learn through this process is that God can take anything you have to tell Him. He is your Father and He can take it.

This particular week was a time when Jamie's mom and dad were visiting with us. We were glad to see them come, and especially for the girls to spend time with them. One moment we were all enjoying each other's company, and then the next moment, as I was preparing dinner, I looked around and Jamie was nowhere to be found. I thought, *That is not like him to leave when his parents are in town.* His dad was inquisitive, asking, "What happened to Jamie? Where did he go?"

This was before cell phones, so I paged him on his pager. He got my page and found a telephone booth and called me, which lets you know how long ago this was. "Jamie, where are you?" I asked.

"Oh, I'm just out looking at property, and I think I have found something."

"What? You do understand your parents are here and your dad is asking about you. By the way, we can't afford any property!"

"I know, we'll talk about it later, I'll see you in a few minutes."

What happened next felt like a blink. We found ourselves getting approved for a loan, moving into this little cottage-like building, and making payments on something we thought we could never rent in a million years, much less own.

I guess you might say, "Wow, Judy, where was your faith?" We had faith, but have you ever been at a point when God pushes you out of your comfortable little nest so you can soar and fly? God knew we were getting ready to soar like the eagles, so, like Jonah, we were tossed into the sea and God said, "Now swim!" That was a big prayer that Jamie had *prayed*, and God *answered* his big prayer, big time!

Some of you reading this right now feel as if you are in a very uncomfortable place and the nest is being stirred and you don't know the reason for the restlessness or the ways things seem to be so distraught on your job, in your business, or your spirit. There is a feeling that something is getting ready to happen and to change, and you know you have been seeking and praying big prayers. Listen, God has moved me to write this book to encourage you to not give up and to keep believing for the bigger, the better, the more, and the greater, because it is coming. The Jeremiah anointing is on you to do *"great and mighty things, which thou knowest not"* (Jer. 33:3). You were made for greatness, you were born for this very moment in time, and you are sprouting some wings because you are getting ready to fly.

As the ministry began to grow and opportunities began to open up, it became apparent that my husband was keeping a little secret from me. I finally got him to confess that he was praying a very huge *until* prayer. He confessed he really wasn't thinking about the little cottage on the hill when he saw all of the property, but what he actually envisioned was the 5,000-square-foot building down the hill. That's really what he saw with his spirit eyes, but he wouldn't tell me because he said, "I knew you couldn't take it then." He was right about that, because at the time I was the one keeping up with the finances in the ministry. I knew what came in, and I certainly knew what went out, and believe me, the budget was tight.

When we moved into the loft building downtown, every month we believed for a miracle to pay the rent, utilities, and the other expenses involved in having your own office space. Now we owned a building with property and all the upkeep that comes along with that.

Jamie has always been the visionary for the ministry, and I'll be honest and tell you his vision always exceeded our budget. One thing we have found out is that when God gives you a vision, He is not checking your bank account. I guess it's that thing we call *faith!* As a matter of fact, we have never had the money to do one single thing we have ever stepped out to do. Every single project that we have started came from vision, and then by God's grace and help we were always rewarded because of our faith and for His glory.

In the middle of all this, our little family's life was shifting and the girls were growing up and changing when the tragedy of 9/11 hit this country and overnight everything changed. Security became a priority at airports, and there were five color-coded levels of terrorist threat established worldwide. Every day when we woke up we really didn't know what level we would be on that day.

If you recall, those days were very precarious. We watched each passenger getting scanned. People were subjected to having wands waved all over their body, and we had to take our coats, belts, shoes, and hats off. Even to this day we are left feeling that we are the criminals in some sense. It was especially hard watching older Americans and children being subject to such scrutiny. The whole process was very unnerving, something we had never had to face before as a nation or the world, and it required patience and endurance from all of us.

I will never forget one instance with Erica at an airport security point. Erica had a little doll that went with us everywhere we would go, and it was quickly falling apart as she would hold on to it in airports, airplanes, long flights, green rooms, and different nations where we would travel.

On one particular trip as we were going through security in those early days after 9/11, her little "pinky" doll was taken away from her by one of the airport security officers. My heart broke just as much as hers, as she cried out for her pinky as they whisked it away from her! She just couldn't grasp with her little one-and-a-half-year-old self why her tiny little baby doll was taken from her to go through some machine.

That day I looked at my husband, and with desperation only a mother can understand I said, "Please, we've got to do something to change this!" Jamie knew there was only one solution, and that was to begin to pursue finding a bus for us to travel on. The girls would be more comfortable, and all of us would be happier knowing that all of these things would be brought to a minimum.

So, we began to pray big prayers again and asked God to send the right bus, the right people, and the right price that we could afford. It would have to be a miracle, but then we serve a miracle-working God. So, we began an *until* prayer.

As we continued to pray big prayers, with God's grace and help we found a beautiful and perfect coach for our family. Another big prayer prayed and another big prayer answered. After some time, it became very obvious that my husband was absolutely right—we did need more space. God was doing so many wonderful things. Lives were being changed, the nations had opened up to us, and many networks were calling us to come and minister on television via satellite TV. Things began to move very rapidly and the demand just kept getting stronger and stronger. Those all-night prayer meetings became a reality now, when it had been just the two of us, praying:

Ask of me, and I shall give thee the heathen for thine inheritance, and the uttermost parts of the earth for thy possession (Psalm 2:8).

You may want to watch what you pray, because you just might get it! We had prayed big prayers, and God had answered those big prayers with big answers. We had, in fact, outgrown the cottage in just a short time. We added more staff and began to explore the possibilities of purchasing the building at the bottom of the hill along with the property that came with it.

As we set aside time for fasting and prayer, God began to speak and we heard so many things begin to rise in our spirits. God began to show us all the possibilities of what He had in mind for this property. He showed us this was to be an institute of mentoring for women from around the world. When I heard the Lord say that to me, I thought, *Lord what did You say?*

He said, "*Yes, Judy, I want you to begin to pour into women the same thing that has been poured into you from your mama, your sisters, your aunts, and powerful women in your life growing up. I want you to begin to share this with women from around the world.*"

Whew! I thought, *Lord, You have got to be kidding me!*

Then I began to remind God of all the things that I am involved in—being on the road, writing books, not to mention two little girls and a husband who needed to be taken care of. He didn't respond in any way except to say, "Okay, just remember, I need you to mentor women."

It was in a large way overwhelming because of what I was already involved in, but I knew that His ways were not my ways, and my thoughts were not His thoughts. I was kind of like Mary, "I pondered these things in my heart" and was really asking myself, *What does this mean, and what will it even look like?*

It really hit home with me when I left on a ministry trip one weekend. At the end of the trip, after ministry, the pastors were walking us to our car. I turned to hug the pastor's wife, and she gently said to me in my ear, "Pastor Judy, I would love for you to consider mentoring me, please." It was almost as if someone had thrown cold water in my face, and really I was stunned. I just looked at her and said, "I will definitely pray about it." God was speaking, and it seemed everywhere I went for the next several weeks and months, that was the question being asked, "Sister Judy, will you mentor me?"

I shared it with Jamie, and he just said to me, "Judy, if that is God, He will continue to give you confirmations of what that will be and what it will look like." Well, that's exactly what God began to do. The vision became more and more clear: *"this is the way, walk ye in it."*

Every day God was showing us over and over what He had in mind. We began to pray about this property and to inquire about it. We got our bubble popped when we learned through a realtor that the asking price was three quarters of a million dollars for the building and the property. Well, I knew that wasn't possible in the natural, but the more we prayed the more we felt this building was meant to be ours, and every time I prayed, that is all I heard, "That is your building! That is your building!" So, we began to pray another big prayer!

One evening while settling down and getting ready for bed, I was taking a bath and praying, and I distinctly heard the Lord say, "Tell them you will give them $260,000 and that's it!" I thought to myself, *Wow! That was a wild thought.* Then I heard and felt that strong thought again: "Tell them you will give them $260,000 and that's it!" I thought, *Whoa! It is true that God does speak the loudest in bath tubs and showers.* Then I proceeded to remind God how much the asking price was: "But Lord, they are asking for $750,000. They will laugh at me!" My complaining to God wasn't getting anywhere. He said again, "Offer them $260,000 and that's it!" God was definitely adamant about that figure because it kept coming up over and over again to me.

I will never forget meeting with the realtor of the property and the building. He was smoking a cigarette in his office that day while laughing at the same time about what God had told me to say. He told me, "Ma'am, just the building is worth $320,000 and that doesn't include the property!" I knew he was telling me the truth because Jamie and I had done our due diligence and had the building appraised. He told us, "The only thing I can do is send you to its owner." I thought, *What a wonderful idea!*

We met the owner on the very property we were believing for and I began to share the vision that God had given to me. He listened very respectively, and when I had shared my heart he looked at me and said, "I want to tell you I know who you are, and I believe in your vision, and let me tell you what I will do. The building is worth $320,000, but I'm going to let you have it for $260,000, and I'm just going to give you the property as a tax write-off." Then he said, "Do you need me to finance it?" Oh, my goodness! Oh, my dear sweet Jesus! You talk about pray until! *Until* prayers are relentless, rowdy, bold, and aggressive. Oh! That was sweet victory! Wow! How great is our God!

The next task was getting started with the actual building, and we saw miracle after miracle that God performed. The one thing that was required in every step was obedience and faith. Every day in my prayer chamber were words that would come forth, and then we would declare truth over everything that God had said to us. It seemed as if miracles were popping up everywhere. The Bible says, *"These signs shall follow them that believe"* (Mark 16:17).

Our first International Institute of Mentoring met together as a group of over 200 people. It was overwhelming, but at the same time we realized quickly we had outgrown the building that we had scheduled to meet in. So, we started building the vision that God had given to us. We had a word from the Lord and we were praying *until* prayers.

I had learned on the other side of faith and obedience, there is always a breakthrough. With a word always comes instruction, and the instruction to Jamie and me was to build this building for the glory of the Lord. The first thing we felt God required of us was to find some fertile soil and get some seed in it.

The next testimony is another example of definitely putting your big prayer into action and seeing how God will give you a *big* answer. One thing I have learned, and I am still learning, is that God sees the end from the beginning. (Remember the train with the engine and caboose?) If you will recall Romans 4:17, He *"calleth those things which be not as though they were."* One thing I love about God is that *"His ways* [are] *past finding out"* (Rom. 11:33).

God doesn't start at the beginning and go to the end. No! What He has ordained has already happened in the spirit realm; we are just waiting for the manifestation on earth of those prayers already answered in Heaven.

One particular week we found ourselves ministering at World Harvest Church with Pastor Rod Parsley for his annual Dominion Camp Meeting. I will never forget that Sunday morning when Dr. Mike Murdock was ministering and raising the offering for Pastor Parsley to buy some new television equipment. Prophetically, Mike Murdock announced, "God has spoken to me that there are one thousand people who are going to give $7,000 to fund the need of the ministry of spreading the Gospel literally around the world through Pastor Parsley's television program, *Breakthrough.*"

I remember Pastor Mike saying, "Now, if that's not you, please bow your head and begin to pray in the spirit for this financial miracle to happen." I remember thinking, *That's certainly not us.* I wasn't feeling $7,000 for an offering while in the middle of a building campaign ourselves, so I just casually began to pray earnestly, asking God to speak specifically to people for this financial miracle for Pastor Rod.

Well, there were some other things happening as I bowed my head. To my utter amazement, my husband was one of the first ones to the front to give the $7,000. I heard Jamie calling me, "Psst, psst, Judy!" I thought to myself as my head was bowed in prayer, *It sounds like someone is calling my name.* Well that someone was Jamie; he had slipped up to the front unbeknownst to me. I was surprised that Jamie had not asked me, "What do you think? Can we pray about giving this $7,000? Are you feeling anything?" Nothing! He was one of the first ones up there.

As I made my way to the front to stand with him, he proceeded to remind me that we were believing for a debt-free building, and because of that we had to find places to plant some really significant seeds. He said, "I believe this is one of them." I'll be honest, that decision blindsided me, and at first I was a little cross with my husband because we didn't get a chance to discuss it, but I trusted him completely and knew God was up to something.

On the way home I was telling the Lord, "Lord what is this going to look like? Now we have planted this large seed and there is another big payment coming up, what are we going to do?" I prayed all the way home trying to stay in faith and just kept believing that all things work together for good. We got home in the wee hours of the morning and there was a message on our answering machine and I thought, *I'll just wait till the morning to see what and who the message is from.* I went to bed with a deep, settled peace that all would be well.

When I woke up the next day, I remember casually making my way to the answering machine and the message was from one of our covenant partners. The message said, "You guys were on my mind this weekend. I wanted to ask you, are you still planning on building the International Institute of Mentoring debt-free? I felt led to go ahead and send you a $100,000 check in the mail. You should get it in a few days." Oh my goodness! You can't believe how very loud it got in our house! Wow! What a big prayer answered! But God still wasn't finished. There was a most beautiful lesson that needed to be learned, and both Jamie and I had a front-row seat.

A couple of weeks after that, we were scheduled to go and minister in a venue, and I remember being sick with a sinus infection so much that I could hardly talk. But somehow, I got through that service by the grace of Almighty God. As we were getting ready to dismiss, our hosts said to us, "We heard about your vision to build a building debt-free and we are trying to do the same thing, so we are supposed to plant $100,000 seed into this work." Oh my! Here we go again! I could hardly contain myself! Here was another *big* answer to prayer bringing the number from a $7,000 seed to a harvest of $200,000.

The next several weeks my birthday was coming up, and to top it off, it was a surprise birthday party. People came from all over to celebrate my 50th Jubilee year. I had two people walk up to me and slip me an envelope and tell me, "Take very good care of this envelope." I knew what that meant. I was curious, so I opened one of them, and there was a $50,000 check in the envelope with a card wishing me a happy birthday. I opened the other one and there was another $50,000 check wishing me a happy birthday. Another *big* prayer answered!

I was floating around all that night; I don't even think I was touching the floor! I can tell you I had a very, very happy birthday and was so thankful for my husband's obedience. Those two checks brought the total sum to $300,000 from a $7,000 seed. Oh, if you will pray big prayers, you will get big answers.

What nobody knew was that God was not only building a place to mentor women from around the world, but also to house a church. Dwelling Place Church International was established in 2011 and continues to meet the needs of our community, region, and the world.

As of this writing, we are enjoying the blessings of the promises of big prayers meeting big answers! Now here's the question: "Are you praying big prayers? If not, why not?" When you do, keep your eyes open, because God will send some good things your way! Remember, Paul said, *"All things work together for the good to those who love Him."*

Your *Pray Until* Challenge

- Are there some big prayers that you have been praying?

- Are you believing for a Jeremiah 33:3 blessing?

- Ask God for the greater instead of the same ole, same ole!

- Write down some big prayers that you would be afraid to tell someone. Then believe God for the big answer!

Note

1. Leslie T. Lyall, *A Passion for the Impossible: The Continuing Story of the Mission Hudson Taylor Began* (London: OMF Books, 1965), 5.

Chapter 6

UNTIL PRAYERS WORK TOGETHER FOR YOUR GOOD

And we know that God causes all things to work together for good to those who love God, to those who are called according to His purpose.
—ROMANS 8:28 NASB

The true purpose of prayer is to get into God's presence so He can outline His agenda for us.
—MARK BATTERSON, *Draw the Circle*

God does nothing but by prayer, and everything with it.
—JOHN WESLEY

*B*ig prayers require big faith! Every time you want God to do something big for you it will always be, as Jesus puts it, *"according to your faith"* (Matt. 9:29). That always involves stretching your faith, expanding your mind, and going the extra mile in believing for the extraordinary. For me, God dropped two special words in my mind for this chapter. See if you identify with them—tweaking and pruning!

I was thinking, "Lord what is it that You want me to say about these words?" I knew the first thing to do was to find the clarity of these words, so I went to the definition in the dictionary. To *tweak* means "to adjust, improve, alter, make adjustments to or change or make modifications." The simplest definition is "making small adjustments for the biggest difference for the most impactful outcome."

What I have learned in my years of "God-tweaking" is that He is very serious about our character and our integrity as His children. The world is constantly watching us—Jesus made sure of that by putting us on top of a hill as the church so that we can be the light in this dark world, and we are also to be the people who are salty to make others thirsty for Him.

I don't know about you, but God has been tweaking me for a long time, and I don't want Him to ever stop. I thank God that He loves me too much to leave me as I am. This tweaking can come in the form of my attitude; improving my gifts; challenging me on my relationships (all of them), my eating habits, my workout habits, my social media use; or in devotion to prayer, fasting, and the study of the Word. Oh yeah! There is a constant tweaking going on in me personally. How about you?

The Bible refers to this tweaking process by saying, *"We...are being transformed into the same image from glory to glory, just as by the Spirit of the Lord"* (2 Cor. 3:18 NKJV). Paul tells us in First Corinthians 13:12:

> *Now we see only a reflection as in a mirror; then we shall see face to face. Now I know in part; then I shall know fully, even as I am fully known* (NIV).

We can only see a small part of the big vision, but God's plan is much bigger and grander than we can imagine. Sometimes it's hard to be under the watchful eye of the Father, but here's what I love about that—we can trust Him that He knows us the best and loves us the most. What we are responsible for is just to trust Him with what we can see and then pray to see more. Solomon said:

I realized that no one can discover everything God is doing under the sun. Not even the wisest people discover everything, no matter what they claim (Ecclesiastes 8:17 NLT).

The good news is, there is always a plan, even for the tweaking. "How do you know this, Judy?" Because I have experienced the tweaking of God many times. Paul told the Church at Philippi:

Therefore, my dear ones...work out (cultivate, carry out to the goal, and fully complete) your own salvation with reverence and awe and trembling (self-distrust, with serious caution, tenderness of conscience, watchfulness against temptation, timidly shrinking from whatever might offend God and discredit the name of Christ).

Here comes the secret!

[Not in your own strength] for it is God Who is all the while effectually at work in you [energizing and creating in you the power and desire], both to will and to work for His good pleasure and satisfaction and delight (Philippians 2:12-13 AMPC).

During this time of seeking the Lord I kept inquiring and questioning the timing of all of this. Charles Dickens wrote, "It was the best of times; it was the worst of times." What was supposed to be one of the greatest highlights of our lives was accompanied by one of the most challenging times of our lives, and in the natural none of it made sense. I was married to a wonderful person, doing what we both loved the most, which was traveling and ministering, and we had two of the most gorgeous little girls in all the world—but to have one of them who wants to die? It did not make sense. So, God began tweaking and pruning us from the inside out.

In the recording studio, tweaking is especially important to perfect your vocal performance for a music project. In technical terms, it's called a "fix." I guess that sounds pretty logical. After all the other tracks have been finished—the keyboards, electric guitar, bass, drums, even the orchestra and background vocals—the last thing I always do is my solo vocal recording. I like to do it last because it is much easier with background vocals and a full orchestra backing up my vocal performance.

When I record, I am usually singing for a producer, my husband, and a couple of engineers. Believe me when I tell you I don't enjoy singing for people who have very keen ears attuned to listen for my mistakes. My favorite thing is hearing the producer say, "Great job! That was perfect; let's do it one more time." If it is perfect, why do I have to do it again? Doesn't make sense to me.

The main job of the people in the control room is to tell me how well I am doing vocally, how to make some improvements, or what to do differently if what I am doing is not working. At the time I may feel I am doing my very best, but then the recording literally tells the truth, the whole truth, and nothing but the truth.

The actual recording doesn't lie. If something is sharp, flat, or off in some form or fashion, time for fixes or tweaking! Before you can move on, you have to make sure everything lines up and is right so that you can move forward with the recording process!

For another example, I can't tell you how many times I have tweaked these chapters that I have written over and over again, and I even recruited other people, after I read them, to read them again and again with fresh eyes. That doesn't even include the editing and tweaking that came later from the editors and staff of Destiny Image Publishers.

What God is showing all of us in this season is that God is doing some incredible things in all of us with shaping and molding. If we will allow Him, He will take us to a place in prayer where there will be some seeking, turning, twisting, and tweaking going on in us and in the entire household of faith. This last season proved to be a time when "anything that could be shaken was shaken."

The other word that came to my spirit was the word *pruning*. When God wants to use someone, He will always begin a pruning process. As a matter of fact, this is what Jesus says about pruning:

> *Every branch in Me that does not bear fruit, He takes away; and every branch that bears fruit, He prunes it so that it may bear more fruit* (John 15:2 NASB).

That is the translation of the New American Standard Bible, but more literally the Greek word means, "He cleanses it." Jesus said:

> *I am the vine, you are the branches, He who abides in Me, and I in him, bears much fruit; for without Me you can do nothing* (John 15:5 NKJV).

85

David shows such tremendous humility as he bows his head in trepidation to God and says, *"Create in me a clean heart, O God; and renew a right spirit within me"* (Ps. 51:10).

Pruning is a very delicate operation—it requires removing dead and dying branches to allow for new growth. When you prune, it deters pests and promotes natural growth, while at the same time it enhances the shape of the plant or tree being pruned. There are different and varied ways to prune, such as:

- Thinning is removing a branch at the point of origin to give more light and penetration.

- Topping involves the top of the central stem of a tree, called the leader, as well as the upper main branches, and it is also used to help a young tree to grow a certain way.

- Raising is trimming low-hanging branches so it will not be obstructive.

- Reduction is trimming a tree's volume for safety reasons.

All new shoots compete with each other, so pruning lets the strong survive while it cuts out the dead, dying, diseased, and damaged branches. *Timing* is also considered to be very important because, during the dormant season before the onset of new growth, those dead branches have to go.

It is imperative that the person doing the pruning has lots of experience. Pruning requires skill, and it requires knowledge of that which is being pruned. A pruner needs to know how the branch ultimately should grow to bring forth the greatest harvest and the most beautiful crop and fruit. On the other hand, an unskilled person who attempts to prune something runs the risk of doing such damage that it could possibly lead to destruction of the thing being pruned.

So when you consider each of these pruning processes individually, you understand why God would use the process of pruning us in order to see our *until* prayers answered. Here is what God showed me about this pruning process as it applies to all of us:

Thinning

The thinning process is used when there are certain people and things that God has to thin out of your life so that you can see only Him. Isaiah said:

> *In the year that king Uzziah died I saw also the Lord sitting upon a throne, high and lifted up, and his train filled the temple* (Isaiah 6:1).

What did you see the year that your best friend left you high and dry? When trouble hit your life? When the pandemic hit? When your spouse left and asked for a divorce? When your loved one passed away? When your child was diagnosed with a sickness or disease? When you had to file bankruptcy?

Isaiah said, *"I saw the Lord."* God loves you enough to thin you out so the only one you see is Him. It's so crucial where your eyes are looking when trouble or pain or unexpected things hit your life. If we are not careful, we will see everything but the Lord.

Topping

Next is the topping process. That's when God will set you right smack down in the middle of spiritual leaders, mentors, and others to help you grow in His way and to bring you to the top of what He has designed for you. Usually it's at a time when you need to hear far more than you want to listen, but it is always wise to listen to wisdom as the truth is spoken to you. I believe that God will send you people who will speak the truth in love because you are at a strategic place in your life where you need miracles, so He will plant you in a place to hear and see the impossible so that you can also bear much fruit.

Raising

Another process is called raising—it is a time when the Spirit of the Lord will get everything out of your sight that would obstruct your view of Him and His will for your life. Don't believe me? Ask Joseph. Joseph dreamed some dreams, but he had to be sold to some Midianites to take him to a kingdom that he would one day be responsible for—literally. This position would be a place where he would eventually be reunited with the family that sold him, and he would save his family from famine. As a result, the whole tribe of Israel would come into existence.

Understand that God is raising you up to take over the very place that was supposed to destroy you. He is making your feet like hind's feet and raising you up so that you can tread on high places.

Reduction

This next one is reduction. Reduction is one none of us enjoy, because we know the Kingdom of God is opposite from the world. In order to go up, you must come down. Whoever wants to be the greatest has to be the servant. Whoever wants to be enlarged has to be reduced.

Moses was on the back side of the mountain when God gave him a command to lead His people out of bondage. He reduced him from being an adopted grandson of Pharaoh to being a shepherd for his father-in-law, Jethro. Sometimes God has to bring us to a place where we realize its *"in him we live, and move, and have our being"* (Acts 17:28).

God will never use anyone unless He sees what they are made out of first. If you feel you are being reduced, you are in good company. Even Jesus was reduced; Paul made it clear:

> *For you know the grace of our Lord Jesus Christ, that though He was rich, yet for your sakes He became poor, that you through His poverty might become rich* (2 Corinthians 8:9 NKJV).

There is a reason you are feeling reduced. It's because God is getting ready to promote you.

Newness

Another process God is using is the newness coming forth. This is a place where only the strong ones who have a firm and solid foundation survive. Everyone can't go where you are going and everybody will not fulfill their purpose completely, but that's when you have to let God do a new thing in you. The old you has to die and the new, strong, and resilient you has to rise up and be the difference maker. Let Him have His way in your *until* prayers! Although Joshua was not one of Moses' sons, God chose him to be Moses' armor-bearer and, more importantly, to lead the children of Israel into the Promised Land. He had to tell Joshua over and over:

> *Only be thou strong and very courageous. ...Have not I commanded thee? Be strong and of a good courage* (Joshua 1:7-9).

God is telling someone, "Be strong and courageous because the Lord your God is with you."

Timing

Then there is the timing process. We have to give God time in our lives to get all of the junk out. Allow Him to do in us all that He needs to do in order to let go of the dead things that are holding us down and stunting our growth so we can produce *until* prayers.

Esther was chosen out of all the women in the land to be the Queen of Persia, and King Ahasuerus loved her more than them all. Because of the horrible ordeal that was placed upon the Jewish nation by the evil Haman, Mordecai, her uncle, reminded Esther of one of the most well-known passages in the Bible, "*Who knows whether you have come to the kingdom for such a time as this?*" (Esther 4:14 NKJV). Never doubt or despise the timing of God in your *pray until* moments.

> *For the vision is yet for an appointed time; but at the end it will speak, and it will not lie. Though it tarries, wait for it; because it will surely come, it will not tarry* (Habakkuk 2:3 NKJV).

Trusting

Last but certainly not least is *trusting the Master Pruner* is working all things together for our good. He knows what He is doing, so let Him have His way.

> *He who has begun a good work in you will complete it until the day of Jesus Christ* (Philippians 1:6 NKJV).

Just as the Word of the Lord came to Jeremiah about the Potter's wheel, in the same manner, He is shaping and molding and making a beautiful vessel out of us; we just have to trust the process.

We have to make sure that we are being led by the Holy Spirit in hooking ourselves up with people of like faith, like destiny, like spirit, and like anointing. If not, the potential for damage is paramount if you allow the wrong person to speak into your life. Allow pastors, teachers, mentors, and mothers and fathers of the faith who have walked this road for a while and who have testimonies of the miracle-working power of God to speak into your life and to build you up in the most holy of faith.

It takes a lot of us to get to the other side of the desired goal of seeing prayer answered. That is why we are called the Body of Christ! It will take all of us—your spouse, your children, your immediate family, your extended family, a pastor, a church family, intercessors, trusted friends, and whoever else you can grab hold of. I don't know about you, but I need all the help I can possibly get when I am in a zone of *until prayer*. In the multitude of counselors there is much wisdom (see Prov. 15:22). Jesus said, "If any two of you agree on earth as touching any one thing it shall be done unto you" (see Matt. 18:19). One of you can put a thousand to flight, and two of you can put ten thousand to flight (see Deut. 32:30).

I remember the time we were walking through one of our hardest seasons of *until*. Our little family was on our way to the airport to drop me off to go on a ministry trip. Jamie was unusually quiet. I was sitting in the back between the girls with both of them holding tightly to my arms and burying their faces in my arms and sides, crying. The tears on my face were hot and dropping very quickly, and I was totally exhausted. Jamie was dealing with exhaustion as well. He was trying to be strong, but I'm sure he was also feeling he needed his wife to stay and help to buffer things that we were facing at the time. We had been apart for a couple of weeks, so to say that we were feeling withdrawals from each other was an understatement. As we were standing there outside the Atlanta Hartsfield Airport saying our goodbyes before I had to leave to catch my flight, all of a sudden God entered into a tweak.

Jamie has his Master's of Divinity degree in marriage and family, so believe me when I tell you he gets the marriage and family thing. He looked at me with this glitter in his eyes and said, "You know what? Why don't we change the ticket so you can fly out a couple of days later. It will cost us some extra money, but we won't have to cancel, and plus, we can spend some extra time together."

Yes! Yes! Yes! That was the tweak that was needed. Lots of cheers went up, and in just a short time everybody was laughing and happy as we got back in the vehicle. He immediately got on the phone, changed my itinerary, and we went on our merry little way, very peaceful with that decision. Yes, thank God for wisdom from my husband. We spent a little money (okay, a lot of money) changing that ticket, but in the end, "All things worked together for the good." Those two extra days helped to resolve a lot of things during that time and also gave us all great quality time together as a family.

God will not always remove all the things that are hard. Sometimes you have to do the hard things and face the music yourself. But I have found that if we will do what we think is hard, He will make the path easier. He will enlarge our territory and make the path that we are traveling on broader so we can keep walking in faith. Reading through the psalms, you can see David talked to himself a lot. There will be many times in your *until* moment when you will have to get up out of that bed, look in the mirror, and encourage yourself in the Lord as David did (see 1 Sam. 30:6). A great example of him talking to himself is found in Psalm 43:5:

Why, my soul, are you downcast? Why so disturbed within me? Put your hope in God, for I will yet praise him, my Savior and my God (NIV).

We may not feel like praising Him in those *until* times, but if we will do it in faith and as the psalmist said, "put your hope in God," then Psalm 18:36 declares, "*You provide a broad path for my feet, so that my ankles do not give way*" (NIV).

God is constantly altering our circumstances, gradually or very suddenly, but the thing I love is that I am at least moving and not standing still.

Sometimes the way gets so narrow that I feel as if I will suddenly fall off the proverbial mountain of faith that I am climbing up, but it is in those moments that my path begins to broaden, my feet are more steady and firm, and I feel more rooted and grounded. The Bible says in Matthew 7:13-14:

Enter ye in at the strait gate: for wide is the gate, and broad is the way, that leadeth to destruction, and many there be which go in thereat: because strait is the gate, and narrow is the way, which leadeth unto life, and few there be that find it.

In this faith walk, when it seems it's getting harder and harder to hold on to our faith and nothing is working out and things are tighter than a rubber band, if we'll hold on to what we know, stay solid, sure, and determined, and stay on the narrow path, then all of a sudden we will notice the path beneath our feet begin to broaden. And just like the children of Israel, He will make a way out of no way. He will make a way in the wilderness, and you will look around and see that your enemies are being swallowed up right before your very eyes. At the end of the day, "All things work together for the good, to those who are the called according to His purpose." Hallelujah!

I'm so glad you are joining me on this journey. Don't quit! By the way, here are some more reasons why you shouldn't quit!

Your *Pray Until* Challenge

- What are some things that you are waiting on to work out?

- Write them down and date them. Give God a time-line and see what He will do with your faith. Remember, "According to your faith, so be it."

Chapter 7

UNTIL PRAYER DOESN'T QUIT

*Therefore do not cast away your confidence, which has
great reward. For you have need of endurance, so that after
you have done the will of God, you may receive the promise.*
—HEBREWS 10:35-36 NKJV

It's a commitment to pray until the prayer is answered.
It's not easy. It requires time. Energy. Sacrifice. It involves
reading and pleading God's promises. It's motivated by
a wholehearted love that's willing to suffer, to repent, to
sacrifice—to do whatever it takes to get an answer.
—ANNE GRAHAM LOTZ, *The Daniel Prayer*

Prayers outlive the lives of those who uttered them, outlive a generation, outlive an age, outlive a world.
—E.M BOUNDS, *Purpose in Prayer*

A promise is something you keep! A promise is something
you hold on to, even when it seems it will never come to
pass. A promise is a vow and a pledge by the one who declares it
with assurance that it will surely come to pass. He assured us in
His Word:

For I am the Lord your God who takes hold of your right hand and says to you, Do not fear; I will help you (Isaiah 41:13 NIV).

With God you are never alone. Never forget—Emmanuel, God with us! I'm not really crazy about the study of math, but if the Bible says, *"I will never leave you or forsake you,"* then know this—God is with us every *nanosecond* of our lives. Do the math and you will learn that a nanosecond actually equals *one-billionth of a second.* Wow! Now that is fast! Paul said in Second Corinthians 1:20-22:

For all of God's promises have been fulfilled in Christ with a resounding "Yes!" And through Christ, our "Amen" (which means "Yes") ascends to God for his glory. It is God who enables us, along with you, to stand firm for Christ. He has commissioned us, and he has identified us as his own by placing the Holy Spirit in our hearts as the first installment that guarantees everything he has promised us (NLT).

Now what does that mean? The Holy Spirit is our counselor, our joy, our peace, our comfort, our teacher, our leader, our guide; He is the promise that Jesus made to His disciples. He told them that it was necessary for Him to go away, for if He didn't go away the Comforter would not come (see John 16:7). He promised that the Comforter would not only be with us but He would be in us (see John 14:17).

What that actually means is that when Jesus was here, He was in fact the Son of Man. He felt what we felt, He cried, He was lonely, He hurt, He was disappointed and discouraged. The Bible says that He is *"touched with the feeling of our infirmities."* The Bible also says that He *"was in all points tempted like as we are, yet without sin"* (Heb. 4:15).

So no one could ever accuse the Son of God of sin, but they could also never accuse Him of not understanding how they felt or feel living here on this earth. Jesus knew and Jesus knows! I'm glad that the Bible says:

> *There hath no temptation taken you but such as is common to man: but God is faithful, who will not suffer you to be tempted above that ye are able; but will with the temptation also make a way to escape* (1 Corinthians 10:13).

Jesus was saying to His disciples, "While I am here on this earth, I have limitations; I can only be in one place at one time." Now we know that Jesus could appear to the disciples walking on the water and other instances, but in essence He was saying, "I am in this earth suit, and while I am here, I have set Myself up to be just like you. But when the Holy Spirit comes, *He will be with you wherever you go.*"

I love the fact that the Father has given us a down payment, in essence, of what Heaven is going to be like. He has given us the gift of the Holy Spirit. Can you imagine what it will be like to walk around Heaven with unspeakable joy, refreshing peace at all times, no temptations or problems, and utter contentment? That is what He has guaranteed us as we walk this earth realm with the Holy Spirit by our side. The Holy Spirit is our down payment of something that is even greater to come.

I remember when I bought my first car. It was a beautiful, brand-new, sky-blue Camaro. I could not believe it was actually mine. My brother Roger was right there with me to walk me through the process of getting this car. My brother, being the sharp businessman that he is, said to the salesperson, "Is this the only one like this on the car lot, sir?"

"Yes," the salesman replied.

My brother looked at me and said, "Well, baby, we had better go ahead and put a down payment on this little baby blue."

I have never heard of that before. I just figured that since I found the car that I wanted, I could tell the salesperson to hold it for me. I said to my brother, "I will go and get my credit approved and just come back and get it."

"No," he said, "that's not how it works in business." He explained, "You see, because it is exactly what you want, and it's exactly how you want it, you don't want anyone coming on the lot when we leave and seeing it and purchasing it before you can get back to get it yourself. That is why we need to put some money down on it—it's called a down payment—to say to the salesperson, 'I am serious about purchasing this car and just to make sure you know just how serious I am, I am securing it. Here is $500 for you to hold and make sure no one else buys this particular car.'"

"Oh, I get it," I responded. What that meant was, when you put a guaranteed down payment on something, it is then reserved for you and held just as if the papers were already signed. It was then that my brother pulled out five crisp $100 bills and handed them to the lady in the office, which meant that this car was as good as mine.

In the same way, Jesus said, "I'm going away, but I'm not going to leave you by yourself. I'm going to send another comforter to you." The reason He did it was to let us know, "I'm coming back for you. And not only am I coming back for you, but while I am gone here is the sweet Holy Spirit for you to enjoy and take comfort in, and you can know this is what it will be like in My presence forever in Heaven." In other words, He gave us the Holy Spirit as a deposit, guaranteeing our full inheritance until we take possession of it.

In His presence we will experience full joy, peace, contentment, and glory of being with Jesus and the Father. Oh, just writing about this makes me homesick for Heaven. I'm so glad that He sent the Holy Spirit. I wouldn't want to live one second without Him.

The greatest example of promises made and promises kept is my mom, who prayed for all of her children to be saved, and God has honored that prayer. All of my family are serving the Lord or are with my mom and dad in Heaven.

I will admit that we were quite concerned for a couple of my brothers who were very far from God at one time. One of my older brothers, Johnny, was away from God most of his life. When my mom was alive here on earth, she would warn my brother of the coming of the Lord and tell him, "Johnny, son, you never know when the Lord will come. He is either coming on the clouds or He will come and get you. Son, you must be prepared to meet Him when He does."

My brother would reluctantly listen and he knew everything that Mama was saying was very true, but he never made a solid decision for the Lord while she was alive. When she went to be with the Lord, Johnny was very much upset and visibly rattled. Nevertheless, his lifestyle did not change. In the natural, it looked like Mama's prayers were not working and were not going to work. However, her prayers didn't quit but were still alive and active.

Then, late one dreadful night on a back road, Johnny was in a car with some of his friends and the car went out of control. The car skidded down into a canal. By chance, or I should say by appointment, God had someone see the car go off into the canal. It was said later that if no one had seen that car go down in that canal, because it was so deep, no one would have known the whereabouts of the people in the car for a while.

The person who saw it happen called the paramedics immediately, and when they got to Johnny, my brother, he was in a very bad situation physically. What was really incredible was that when the paramedic saw Johnny, she knew exactly who he was. She proceeded to call my older brother, Sam, and in the middle of the night she woke him up to tell him that Johnny has been in a very serious accident. She let him know that they were on the way to the hospital and he might want to meet them there to see him.

My brother Sam got dressed and left immediately for the hospital. Just as he stepped into the emergency room, there was my brother being wheeled into the ICU on a gurney. Sam was able to grab hold of Johnny's hand, and while they were working on him Sam was able to pray and lead him to the Lord. Sam asked Johnny to squeeze his hand if he received Jesus into his heart; in response, Johnny squeezed Sam's hand for the last time implying, "Yes, I receive Jesus now as my Lord and Savior." They took him away, and not long after that Johnny lost consciousness and never regained it. I believe he was united with Jesus and my mama in that instant, and her *until* prayers had certainly been answered because she refused to quit. It reminds me of the story of the thief on the cross beside Jesus, who said, "Remember me when You come into Your Kingdom." Jesus told him, "This day you will be with Me in paradise" (see Luke 23:43).

That is why someone who is reading this book now can't give up praying for your prodigal son, daughter, husband, wife, friend, or anyone else you have a promise for. It is never too late for God to answer your prayers. As long as there is breath, there is hope. Your prayers never quit, even after you live out your days. God is a God of the second, third, fourth, and however many chances. He will do everything to bring many sons and daughters to Himself. Always remember this—God cannot restore if you give up.

Solomon said, *"Better is the end of a thing than the beginning"* (Eccles. 7:8). You can't judge where you are right now by what you see, feel, or hear; it has to be strictly judged by the Word of the Living God. Isaiah 46:10 says that God declares the end from the beginning.

Here is what that verse looks like. You get a word from the Lord through a promise God has declared in His Word from a prophet, a pastor, friend, or a God dream. You know it is a God word! A God moment! God will always show you the future of a God word. It may be a day vision or night vision; it may be a daydream or a night dream, but whatever it is, you have the vision in front of you and you can visibly recall every minute detail of it. Sometimes the ability to recall specific details about a dream or a vision is one way you can know something is from God. It's like you can see into the future through the spirit and you can actually visualize that son or daughter living for God and serving Him. Then you come back into the now, or natural, and you have memories of what you saw coming forth in the future. The important thing to do when you see a vision from God is to begin to declare what you saw in the future and what was ahead of you to come forth in the natural realm. When you begin to declare what is ahead of you, then it automatically begins to make a way for that dream or vision that God gave to you to come to pass in the natural.

That's why you have to be careful who you share your dreams and visions with. I can't share some of my deepest revelations from God with just everybody. You have to find people of like faith, like spirit, like destiny, and like anointing to share your secrets from God with. In that way, they can help you to call them forth in the supernatural. And here is why. When you share something that has to happen in the supernatural, people will think that the beginning has to show up first. No! It doesn't work that way. God says, "I declare the end from the beginning."

For example, the young boy David prophesied to Goliath exactly what he was going to do in First Samuel 17:

> *This day the Lord will deliver you into my hands, and I'll strike you down and cut off your head. This very day I will give the carcasses of the Philistine army to the birds and the wild animals, and the whole world will know that there is a God in Israel. All those gathered here will know that it is not by sword or spear that the Lord saves; for the battle is the Lord's, and he will give all of you into our hands* (1 Samuel 17:46-47 NIV).

Wow! That sends goosebumps up my spine as I think of the boldness and the authority that this young boy spoke with, and with God's help he did exactly as he had prophesied he would do. Look at the next couple of verses:

As the Philistine moved closer to attack him, David ran quickly toward the battle line to meet him. Reaching into his bag and taking out a stone, he slung it and struck the Philistine on the forehead. The stone sank into his forehead, and he fell facedown on the ground. ...David ran and stood over him. He took hold of the Philistine's sword and drew it from the sheath. After he killed him, he cut off his head with the sword (1 Samuel 17:48-51 NIV).

Oh hallelujah! Just like that, David fulfilled every word he prophesied to Goliath, the giant. I want to tell you to prophesy to your children, to your marriage, and to believe for the impossible to happen. Your words are powerful! You just have to keep proclaiming what you saw in the future to make a way and a road to the place that you have already seen. Before you know it, what you spoke will become flesh; the manifestation of it will actually stand in front of you as a testimony of what the Lord has done. I have often said if you say it you will see it, and if you're not saying it then you won't see it.

In 2020, my older brother, Sam—who led my brother Johnny to Jesus on his deathbed—went to be with the Lord after a long battle with lung cancer. I know that there was such a great reunion for the two brothers being together now for eternity. This past year in 2021, my middle brother, Jerry, also went to be with the Lord. I am so joyful to report that God saved him right before he left this world because my mama had a promise from God and He certainly would not go back on His word.

Jerry was not just my middle brother but he was also the middle child in a family of 12, right smack dab in the middle. I know oftentimes people who find themselves in that birthing order feel unseen and unheard. That was my brother in some ways. It was not necessarily anyone's fault, but I'm sure he had to fight to maintain his position.

I don't remember a lot of things about my brother because of our age difference. One of the fondest memories I had as a child was when he would walk in the room where my sister, Mary Lonnie, and I were watching cartoons, and he would sit and watch them with us. Oftentimes, our older brothers would come in and change the channel to watch a football or baseball game, but not Jerry. He was sweet like that.

When he was 16 years of age, he quit school and moved to the big city of Charlotte, North Carolina. My mama instructed one of my older sisters who lived there, Sylvia, to look out for him, and she did until the day he died. Jerry was someone who was very close to my mom, and he was also a very comical person. He loved to laugh and he loved to make others laugh, and he would often do it at his own expense. He truly loved people and I know he loved God. When he left home, my mama didn't want him to, but he had made up his mind that he wanted to go and make a life for himself, but we also knew he really hated farm work. There wasn't anything anyone could say to talk him out of it, so my mama committed him to the Lord, as she did all of her other children, and sent him on his way.

The big city proved to be good to Jerry as he progressed, and it was great to see him come home in his big city clothes with stories about his job, but there was something missing in Jerry's life, and that was a relationship with God.

He met a girl and they got married. Not too long afterward two little boys came along, and the demand to be a good father and provider became paramount for him. The little family moved into a pretty little house. He was driving a good truck and there was a car for the rest of the family, but the burden of *things* began to weigh him down, so he got another job working a different shift. It was a hard time carrying a heavy load of working two jobs and two shifts week in and week out.

One night he went to his second shift job and he was having a really hard time staying awake and someone on the job introduced him to crack cocaine. His life spiraled down a very horrible path from that night on. At the end of that path he lost everything. He lost his family relationships, his jobs, his house, car, truck, and before long he found himself homeless—living on the streets, waiting for the next time he could get a fix of this drug straight from the pits of hell. He would do anything to fill the craving for this addiction, and often my sister, Sylvia, found herself bailing him out of jail.

I wish this was a fairy-tale story, but for 40 years my brother was in and out of drug rehabs, halfway homes, and on the streets struggling to survive. Many times, our family would try to intervene and talk some sense in his head, but there was nothing that penetrated his mind except this addiction demon that had a tremendous hold on him.

For one brief moment, he gave his heart to the Lord, moved back home, and stayed with my sweet sister Alice. Alice was a godsend for Jerry—she cooked for him, bought him clothes, and did everything that she and the rest of the family could do to help him get back up on his feet, only to be told several months later that he missed "the big city lights" and he needed to go back "home." As a grown man, there was nothing that anyone could do. But there was one thing that was playing a tremendous part in all of this, and that was my mama's *until* prayers, which would not quit. Although she had gone to be with the Lord, her prayers were still very much alive, and I can tell you that she prayed many times for Jerry and his family and God had heard every one of her prayers.

It wasn't long before we learned that he was on the streets again. But this time the outcome was quite different. The Bible says:

> *Be not deceived; God is not mocked: for whatsoever a man soweth, that shall he also reap* (Galatians 6:7).

The reaper was showing up more frequently than ever before in Jerry's life. The coronavirus had hit and the people on the streets were suffering terribly. He found himself in a hospital with COVID, pneumonia, and later on he suffered from a stroke that left him paralyzed and unable to walk. He was very distraught and unhappy being in a healthcare facility, getting therapy every day to no avail.

When we went to visit him in that hospital, he told the family, "I have spent my life and wasted it, and now I am ready to go home to Heaven. My heart is right, and I have forgiven and I've asked God to forgive me, and now I am ready." Jerry had made up his mind that he was done with this ole world and he just wanted to go home to Heaven.

The doctors informed us that it wouldn't be long before Jerry would be gone. Those last days were filled with our family praying over him, singing hymns to him, and just loving on him. The assurance that everything was right between his soul and his Savior was such a blessing for our family. After 72 years, we knew where he was, and all was well with his soul. Jerry did make that journey. The last thing he said to one of my siblings was, "I am ready now! It's time for me to go home to see Mama and Daddy and Jesus," and that's what he did. Never, ever underestimate the power of *until* prayer. *Until* prayers never quit!

The Bible has promised us 70 or maybe 80 years here on this earth, and it describes this life as a vapor and then it's gone (see James 4:14). But eternity is infinite. So we will have eternity to be with our Lord and our family and catch up on lost time. That is why it is so crucial that you never quit praying, you never stop believing, and you never stop reminding your loved ones of the glories of Heaven to gain and the hotness of hell to shun. Just keep right on declaring what God has said about those you love.

Joshua Christmas was a powerful young man, the son of Pastor Kent Christmas from Regeneration Church in Nashville, Tennessee. Josh was raised in a pastor's home in Washington State, but something tragic happened to him at the age of five years old, unknown to his parents—he was molested by a neighbor. It dramatically changed the trajectory of his life. Then when he turned eight his parents divorced, and that left a big hole in Joshua's heart. Because of what he endured and the cards that had been dealt him, he was a very confused young boy growing up.

At 12 years old he went to live with his dad and his stepmom, Candy Christmas. There he got really involved in their church as he struggled to find his identity. He found himself participating in everything that the church offered, thinking that if he would do that, it would help with his thoughts and insecurities. But the more involved he got, the more he found himself dealing with a great amount of anxiety and depression as he was struggling with same-sex attraction. At one point he confessed to his dad and another pastor the struggle he was having. He thought if he could expose how he felt in the light, it would help to dispel the darkness in the very pit of his soul, but nothing changed.

At 21 years of age, Josh made the decision to pursue a homosexual lifestyle. He moved out and got his own apartment and began a downward spiral into a lifestyle that would eventually lead him into drugs, alcohol, and just pure misery. With no communication with any of his family, Josh sank deeper and deeper into isolation, rebellion, and running from everyone who loved him. But on the other end of the spectrum, there was a father who would not give in or give up on his son. Pastor Kent kept praying, fasting, declaring, and decreeing what the Word said about Joshua.

As a slave to the deception of his lost identity and hopelessness, Josh turned to pills to help him to cope. He tells how God would not let him die, even when it seemed against all odds that he would live after overdosing many times.

Joshua found himself in a relationship with a man he was later engaged to, and they were making plans to be married. He tells the story of how he was driving home from a gay pride parade and he turned the radio on and for the first time he heard Carrie Underwood's song, "Jesus, Take the Wheel." He felt so empty and lost and really cried out to God as the lyrics were penetrating his heart.

When he got home that night, he just felt like he wanted to hear some good Gospel hymns, so he went to YouTube and began to listen to the great hymns of old. As he listened, something happened—the presence of God entered the room, and right there on the floor in his living room, he knelt and cried out to God.

The next day, he went to church. One of the greatest worldwide evangelistic voices of our lifetime, Reinhard Bonnke, was ministering that day, and there in the balcony, sitting by himself, Josh asked Jesus to cleanse him and forgive him and come into his heart. *Instantly,* he was delivered and set free in that very moment.

God began to use anointed people to minister to Josh to bring total healing to his life, and he began a journey of wholeness. While visiting a church years later, God sent Carrie, a beautiful young woman, into his life to love and honor him and to minister alongside of him. In addition, God also gave him two perfect little boys.

Josh was home, saved, free, and delivered and began using his gift as a culinary chef to serve The Bridge Ministry, founded by Candy Christmas, his stepmom.

The last time I saw Josh minister was at my husband's men's conference. I remember how very powerful and passionate he was in sharing his testimony of the miracle-working power of God that had set him free. That night I saw men of all ages weep and crumble under the presence of God as he shared the message of hope and deliverance and how God could do the same for them.

Things changed on a very cold day in January, 2022 when Josh suffered a brain bleed and was put on life support. The whole world prayed for Josh, for the family, and for his miracle, but God saw fit to heal him His way. So on Sunday, February 6, 2022, Josh finished his course. I will never forget one of the last things Pastor Kent said as he was speaking over his son at his memorial service: "I just thank God that He brought him back home, and that he didn't die gay!" God heard that dad's prayers and the family's prayers and God heard Josh's prayer.

In his testimony, Josh always encouraged parents, family, and friends to never give up on your loved ones. God will always hear your prayers. What would Pastor Kent say? *Never give up!*

What would my mama say? *Never give up!*

What would God have me say to you in these last words in this chapter? *Never give up!*

Pray this prayer right now!

> *Father, I thank You because You are giving me the strength to never give up! So I declare:*
>
> *I will not give up.*
>
> *I will never give up.*
>
> *I will in no way give up.*
>
> *I will by no means give up.*
>
> *As a matter of fact, I will find it impossible to give up. I am not capable of giving up. Because of that I will simply refuse to give up. In the name of Jesus I renounce any thought of ever giving up.*

Here's another one:

> *I will not listen to those who tell me to give up—not now, not ever. Instead, I will pray until!*
>
> *Why? Because there is a convergence coming!*

Your *Pray Until* Challenge

- Are you willing to pray until?
- What disappointments have you walked through? Did you stay steadfast?
- Are you at peace with God even if you have faced storms?

Chapter 8

CONVERGENCE OF GOD MOMENTS

Your word is a lamp to my feet and a light to my path.
—PSALM 119:105 NKJV

Direction that comes from God's Word is both immediately at hand and revelatory of that which is distant.
...You'll have a flashlight in one hand and a giant spot-
light in the other. Both aspects of my pathway come into
view: details for today and discernment for tomorrow.
—JACK W. HAYFORD[1]

I love words; I love the study and meaning of words. I have always
been curious about meanings and their origins. I participated
in a spelling bee at some time in my young life; I didn't win, but I
really enjoyed the challenge of it. In this chapter, I am eager to tell
the story of timeframes, segments of time, and sequences of time
in my story with Jamie and, of course, the girls.

Recently in a conversation with my husband, we got to talking
about our story of coming together as a husband and wife, and
about all the God moments that had to happen to literally bring us

together. I had to come into agreement with my purpose and God's plan to see my *until* moment come to pass and to see those prayers that I had prayed converge into one glorious moment in time.

In our conversation together the word *convergence* came up. This word is really interesting to me. *Convergence* is "the act or process of converging; the tendency to meet in one point, the act of coming together, to move toward or meet at one point." An example is a river converging with another river and joining as one.

For things to converge properly, everything has to work out in proper sequence. For example, in order for two people to converge or come together, or two situations to converge and be compatible, events and sequences need to take place in the natural and in the supernatural.

I found this old internet meme recently and wanted to start this chapter off with it, because it demonstrates this idea of convergence:

Ancestral Mathematics

In order to be born, you needed:

- 2 parents
- 4 grandparents
- 8 great-grandparents
- 16 second great-grandparents
- 32 third great-grandparents
- 64 fourth great-grandparents
- 128 fifth great-grandparents
- 256 sixth great-grandparents

- 512 seventh great-grandparents
- 1024 eighth great-grandparents
- 2048 ninth great-grandparents

For you to be born today from 12 previous generations, you needed a total of 4,094 ancestors over the last 400 years.

Think for a moment—how many struggles? How many battles? How many difficulties? How much sadness? How much happiness? How many love stories? How many expressions of hope for the future?—did your ancestors have to undergo for you to exist in this present moment?

These stats are really overwhelming to consider; nevertheless, they are true. A lot of things have to happen in order for convergence to occur. Here's a passage I love to go to when considering convergence and those seemingly complicated and pesky parts of life that get a little fuzzy.

O Lord, you have examined my heart and know everything about me. You know when I sit down or stand up. You know my thoughts even when I'm far away. You see me when I travel and when I rest at home. You know everything I do. You know what I am going to say even before I say it, Lord. You go before me and follow me. You place your hand of blessing on my head. ...You made all the delicate, inner parts of my body and knit me together in my mother's womb. ...You saw me before I was born. Every day of my life was recorded in your book. Every moment was laid out before a single day had passed (Psalm 139:1-5,13,16 NLT).

What a comfort to know that even though things may get complicated, God's thoughts are more powerful and His plan is perfect. Nothing happens by chance, and there is a timeframe to the doings of God and we can trust Him with those.

When I entered college at the age of 24, I really wasn't seeking a relationship with anyone. I was interested only in traveling and ministering around the world. I was still young and wanted to make my mark on the Kingdom of God and see lives changed. As the years began to pass, one of the most dreadful things happened to my family—my mom went home to be with the Lord. I was devastated at the news. My very best friend in all the world and my most loyal prayer partner had gone on to her eternal reward, and although I was joyful for her that she had finished her course, it left a big hole in my heart.

For the first time in my life, I felt loneliness that I had never experienced. It was then that I felt the need to actually start praying for a husband and family. I would dream about what it would be like to be married and to have a husband, some children, and to own a home and to be settled down. These kinds of thoughts were normally not me at all.

It was around 1986 when my prayers began to intensify for me to find Mr. Right. I believed that all things work together for good to those who are the called, and so I began to do weekly fasts calling my husband in. I believed in the scripture, *"Write the vision, and make it plain upon tables, that he may run that readeth it"* (Hab.

2:2). I knew the important things I was looking for and believing for in a husband, and I was continually telling God about them.

One day during one of my prayer times, I began to realize what would actually have to happen in order for the Spirit to lead him directly to me by a convergence. It was like God just opened up my spirit and began to give directives exactly how to pray. I was mesmerized by what the Spirit of God revealed to me.

In this chapter I want us to look very diligently at all the things that happen in order for prayer to be answered. The Bible says:

In the beginning, God created the heaven and the earth. And the earth was without form, and void; and darkness was upon the face of the deep. And the Spirit of God moved upon the face of the waters (Genesis 1:1-2).

Then something extraordinary began to happen—God began to speak. The Bible goes on to say God spoke and said, "*Let there be light: and there was light*" (Gen. 1:3). It was then that it seemed as if things began to move.

Then God divided the light from the darkness. He called the light *day* and the darkness *night*. Next God divided the two firmaments, and one He called Heaven and the other was earth. Then God began to call forth the earth to produce grass and herbs and fruit. God then made two great lights, the one to rule by day and the other to rule by night, and He made the stars also. Watch what happens:

And God said, Let the waters bring forth abundantly the moving creature that hath life, and fowl that may fly above the earth in the open firmament of heaven. And

God created great whales, and every living creature that moveth, which the waters brought forth abundantly, after their kind, and every winged fowl after his kind: and God saw that it was good (Genesis 1:20-21).

God didn't stop there. Next came the cattle, and then things that creep on the ground. Can you imagine every bug, insect, and species known to mankind as they began to crawl, maneuver, and squirm on the earth and in the sea? On and on God just kept creating, and by the way, He is still creating. Then finally we get to verse 26:

And God said, Let us make man in our image, after our likeness: and let them have dominion.

Here is what I want you to notice. God didn't create the fish until there was a sea for them to inhabit. He didn't create all the land animals until there was land. He spoke and said, *"Let the waters bring forth abundantly"* (Gen 1:20) because He knew those whales and sea creatures were going to need something to eat, and that is why He called forth an "abundance" of them all. God is a god of order and timing—perfect timing.

Then He had to have someone in the earth to take care of all that He created, so He brought forth Adam and Eve. The interesting thing about that is, God couldn't bring Adam and Eve until there was an earth for them to inhabit. After it was all said and done, He rested on the seventh day and said, *"It is good!"*

If God was so meticulous about creation, you have to know that He cares so much more for our lives. Even now, He is creating order even when it seems chaotic. Our job is just to pray until we see that order begin to line up and converge.

Have you read through the book of Exodus lately? God was so meticulous about the building of the Ark of the Covenant, the Tabernacle, and creating the anointing oil, etc. I can tell you, He is serious about order for our lives as well. What I have found out in this life that I have lived so far is that a lot of things have to happen first before something else happens.

I know there are some things God will skip over, because that is how He planned it. For instance, have you ever heard of people meeting one week and the next week they're married? Or a business deal that just all of a sudden happens? It's like it just falls into someone's lap and there is no rhyme or reason for it to happen—it just does! Then there are other things that fill episode after episode, drama after drama, and there is a struggling and a wrestling to make things happen in order to bring certain things forth.

In the Kingdom, there are God moments when God sets you up simply to bring a God convergence to your life. You can't explain it except to say, *"That was a God thing!"*

When I left home to pursue the call of God on my life, God sent me to a little town in eastern Tennessee by the name of Cleveland. I attended a private college, Lee University, and was just trying to make decent grades, going to the library, chapel during the week, and church on the weekends. Wednesday nights were Bible study at a local church I attended, and I would go to any other services I could find. I had many doors open up as I joined the campus choir and also began to sing more and more in our chapel services as a soloist.

When I would go to church on Sundays, there was a college recruitment group I loved to hear. I loved it when they would be in town ministering. I had never seen this group sing before I moved to Tennessee. When I went to this church they would sing and the anointing on them was so powerful that my heart would yearn to be a part of something like that. I just couldn't envision myself singing with such a dynamic group as this one, but God was working and convergence and prayer were at work.

I never dreamed that one day I would be asked to audition for this particular group, but that is exactly what happened. There were a lot of things that had to take place to get things moving, and this group was the beginning of that chapter in my life.

One particular day I was in a local restaurant when the director of this group, who was also the minister of music of the church where I attended, walked up to me and invited me to come and minister on a Wednesday night. At the time, I didn't know he was planning on auditioning me for the group, but he was, and I was definitely up for a God moment.

You have to always keep your spiritual antennas up because the enemy is always there to abort the plan of God for your life. At the beginning of my sophomore year, my grades weren't exactly as I would have desired for them to be, so the enemy sent a person in a high position of my department to tell me, "I don't think you're going to make it; it might be best for you to go back home." It was like a dagger had been cut through my heart. On the other hand, with that dagger came a determination that said, "Hell will have to freeze over now before I go back home and go back on what God has spoken over my life." It was God who had spoken to me and told me to leave home and study music and the ministry, and by faith that is exactly what I had done. The last thing on my mind was listening to the voice of defeat trying to make me quit and move back home.

The moving parts were now intensifying. It started with me moving to Cleveland, Tennessee. It was very difficult for my mom and me to be separated because I was the child of her old age, like Joseph was for Jacob. It was very difficult for our family, and I greatly missed the church that I was a part of.

As I was preparing to move to Tennessee, there was a lady from our region who felt led to come to our house and speak to me. She was considered a very godly person in our community, and she was, but her word was off-kilter with what I knew God had said to me. She basically said that if I left I would do it out of disobedience, and many people would suffer. Well, I knew that I had a word from the Lord that I had to leave and study ministry. I knew that I wasn't in disobedience, but what I was carrying was not just for a particular church or a particular people. What I was carrying was for the nations of the earth.

In every one of our lives there comes a supernatural order, which is one of the reasons why we counsel our daughters, Kaylee and Erica, "Don't rush the process of God. You have to wait on the Lord, because if you get out of order, chaos will ensue, and you will miss the plan and mess up what God has planned all along." Hosea said if you sow the wind, you will reap the whirlwind (see Hos. 8:7).

Let me ask you a question—what happens if you miss the perfect will and plan of God? I'll tell you what will happen. God will have to fix it all and bring order again. It will all have to be realigned, if at all possible; if not, then you birth an Ishmael, not an Isaac.

Because of so many Ishmael decisions and our inability to wait on the Lord and have patience and do what the Word says, everything gets out of sequence and out of order. When that happens there comes pandemonium and chaos. Unfortunately, that is the reason why so many families in our churches are going through so much chaos—because they weren't willing to wait on the Lord.

David said, *"Wait on the Lord: be of good courage, and he shall strengthen thine heart: wait, I say, on the Lord"* (Ps. 27:14). I waited until Jamie came into my life, and looking back, I am glad that I did. I daily renewed my heart. I could have aborted the plan of God, but I chose to wait on God.

Whenever I look back now at some of the people I thought might be good recruits for a husband, I shiver at the thought of being married to one of them. I would think, *Well how about this one, God? Maybe this person, he's a preacher?* I look back now at those same people, and I know those people weren't God's best for me. The opportunities for relationships were right there in front of me if I would have pursued them. I could have said, "I'm going to make this work, it will be okay; I'll just have to work a little extra hard." But I'm so glad that God did not let me mess up my life or my girls' lives. I'm glad I waited for Jamie. If we will trust Him, through His grace we will find the right path.

It was in the oracles of God, the way that my life and Jamie's meshed together. There had to be a meeting for things to work out, situations had to happen and change, circumstances had to come into alignment for the perfect will of God to unfold.

On Jamie's end, he was also praying for convergence with the wife with all of the qualities he had written down. He asked God for someone with dark skin, dark hair, someone who can sing, and especially someone who had a heart to pray as fervently as his mom prayed. Our paths converged one hot day in Atlanta, Georgia at

So convergence is happening all over the place, and like David I was the least likely, yet God had other things in mind. I had no plans of going to college because I didn't have the grades. I didn't have the want-to either. We weren't even a Pentecostal family; we weren't a family of *until* prayers. It wasn't until my mama was baptized in the power of the Holy Ghost that things began to radically change in our lives. My family, all of them, grew up as people who attended an independent Baptist church. We were there by tradition because all of our ancestors attended there all of their lives.

One day, something wonderful happened to Grandma Lonnie. She experienced a convergence that changed everything in our lives. There was a tent meeting in our area—I'm talking about the kind of meeting with the sawdust on the ground—and my grandma sneaked off to see if she could find out what all the fuss was about. That night she received the baptism of the Holy Spirit with the evidence of speaking in an unknown tongue. She was radically changed by the power of the Holy Spirit, never to be the same again.

You see, *until* prayers are birthed out of a Pentecostal experience and an awakening encounter of real fire and real hunger, and my grandma was a candidate for both of them. However, my grandfather didn't want anything to do with Pentecost. As a matter of fact, he was convinced that my grandmother had gone to this meeting, and someone had sprinkled some kind of dust on her, and it had affected her mind. No! Absolutely not! My grandma had come into a divine experience with God, and it had made such a powerful impact on all of us as she operated in such an anointing with healings and miracles that it even changed generations.

I remember as a young child, my mom would lay her hands on me and would transfer what God had given to her through her mother, and I can tell you, it was powerful and real. My mom came through the lineage of *until* prayers, I came through a generation of *until* prayers, and now my girls understand and operate in *until* prayers.

As I write this book, there is not one doubt in my mind that the devil sent a spirit of fear to destroy Kaylee and to snuff her out and even convince her to kill herself as an eight-year-old. She didn't know how she would even do it; he just tortured her and tried to convince her that this was the best way out of her tortuous fear. I'm so glad that God is smarter than the enemy, because without that experience and victory Kaylee could never be who she is right now. I really believe that God said, "I need for your family to understand that this is going to be very painful, but I need for you all to go through this together and get to the other side so that you can help other families."

Jesus said to His disciples, "I need to go through Samaria." There was someone waiting for Him to get to Samaria who needed the Gospel message that He had to give. On the other side of Jesus doing what the Father was prompting Him to do, there was a convergence going on. The road to Samaria was a bitter road where He would be hated as soon as someone saw Him there, but to Jesus it would be worth it.

Some of you are wondering why you are going through some things right now and feel as if you are going through a Samaria. You're thinking, *Why am I going through this dark place? Why does my marriage seem to be so shaky?* Even Jesus had to go through some things and some areas that He didn't want to. In the same way, God always has someone waiting on you to go through the hard way, not the easy one.

You can't despise your *until* prayers because you are in the middle of your convergence. If you make a choice to turn before the GPS instructs you to, you'll make the wrong turn and there is no telling how long you will be on the wrong road endlessly driving. The best thing to do is to stay on the road that is marked the right way, and don't get off. Stay on the road of faith! Stay on the road of *pray until!*

If you get off the road of faith, you are making a choice to abort the real plan of God. You don't want your life to be an Ishmael because of your stubbornness, unwillingness to listen, and unwillingness to wait for your *until* prayer to be answered.

This is what I know about Kingdom convergence—it is a "pow" moment. When I say a "pow" moment, what I mean is, it is like an explosion, like a gun going off. It is like an announcement. It announces a supernatural happening from a supernatural place manifesting in a natural area. When we say, "God, Your Kingdom come on earth as it is in Heaven," we are pleading, yet giving God permission to bring convergence on the earth.

Again, convergence is where two entities come together to become one. It's the marriage of a man and a woman. Convergence is the conception of a seed—literally a sperm and an egg.

When conception takes place, there is a spark or shot of light that takes place in the body. Scientists can't explain it, and they don't understand it, but they have seen this spark or this light that happens at conception. I can tell you it is a God-biological convergence. That convergence of the sperm of my father and the egg of my mom at 46 years old was a miracle. What is so wonderful is that out of the 200 to 300 million sperm that were competing against me, swimming upwards to meet the ovum, only 300 to 500 actually reach the site while the others get tired on the way because it's not an easy race. Of the 300 that do manage to reach the egg, only one fertilizes it.

In this case, the winning one was me!

Watch this!

You ran a race without your eyes and legs and you won.

You ran a race without your education and you won.

You ran without a certificate and you won.

You ran without help and you won.

What makes you think you will lose now?

Now we have the knowledge of God's Word, so don't give up on God's plans, visions, and dreams that He has for you. Giving up now is an insult to your Creator.

It doesn't matter what you see now. Take it as a challenge and always remember that you won from the womb and you will win this present battle. I made it! It was a Kingdom convergence. Kingdom convergence is where God's will and purpose are ignited by manifestations.

The week after our honeymoon, Jamie felt the need to do a new recording, but he wanted to contact one of the biggest producers in the music industry at the time—Lari Goss. We knew the reputation of Lari because of who he had produced back in the day, such as Sandi Patti, Larnelle Harris, and Brooklyn Tabernacle Music. We felt led to call Lari and to inquire if he would be interested in working with us. We were in the in-between and we were floating as newlyweds, and yet I was between a closed door and believing for an open door. As we talked with him, we all knew that something was happening in the spirit realm, and it proved to be true. That phone call led to ten recordings with Lari Goss. Oh my goodness, the songs, the music, the arrangements, the orchestra, and relationships that led to doors upon doors I never anticipated in ministry. That moment on the phone with Lari in our small condominium was a Kingdom convergence moment. It was a spark, a "pow," that led us in so many directions.

When we presented Lari with the song "Days of Elijah," we didn't know what God had planned for that song. He listened to only a demo of the song and his immediate response was, "Guys, this song will be *that* song." Now we know the rest is history! It was another Kingdom convergence that would lead me to sing thousands of times in many countries where I would sit with presidents, prime ministers, and even share the Gospel in Muslim countries where people were moved by the anointing on the music. That one Kingdom convergence led us from the in-between through a door that I would never have anticipated, and still today that door remains open and fulfilling.

My convergence didn't happen overnight like I would have wanted it to. Sometimes there is a hallway between the open and the closed door, which I call the in-between. Are you ready to step out of the hallway into that open door?

Your *Pray Until* Challenge

- Do you feel you are in a convergence right now?
- Begin to pray a "Your Kingdom come, Your will be done on earth as it is in Heaven" prayer, and be specific.

Note

1. Jack W. Hayford, *Living the Spirit-Formed Life* (Bloomington, MN: Chosen Books, 2017), 110.

Chapter 9

THE IN-BETWEEN MOMENTS

I will give him the key to the house of David—the high-est position in the royal court. When he opens doors, no one will be able to close them; when he closes doors, no one will be able to open them.

—ISAIAH 22:22 NLT

The altar is the only place where what you have been can be interrupted by what you can become!

—PAT AND KAREN SCHATZLINE,
Rebuilding the Altar

When you are contending for your *until* moment, you will find yourself in some in-between moments. Notice in this scripture in Isaiah there are two doors that God is talking about here—an open door and a closed door. Obviously, there is an in-between of the two. Each door represents a season of a person's life. You have a current season and then you have a coming season. So you have present times and you have approaching times.

We all get tired in our current season. The current season is a time of the same ole, same ole! There is nothing new happening, not even on the horizon as far as you can see, so you feel stuck, nothing moving forward and nothing moving backward—you're just stuck! This is the time when we need the grace of patience and endurance, which no one likes. You will be the most tempted to quit when you are the closest to your calling, to your open doors, and to answered prayer. But here's the thing—quitting only leaves you with the memory of unrewarded labor. If I am going to have a memory, I want it to be rewarding, not unrewarded.

Always remember the instruction given to us in Habakkuk 2:2-3:

> *Then the Lord said to me, "Write my answer plainly on tablets, so that a runner can carry the correct message to others. The vision is for a future time. It describes the end, and it will be fulfilled. If it seems slow in coming, wait patiently, for it will surely take place. It will not be delayed"* (NLT).

There are times when we want the old to pass away, and we want the new right now. We don't want to wait for the next season. However, God doesn't operate like that. There are lessons to be learned in the hallway of mundane and misery. Most of those times we feel rejection or we feel as if God is not hearing us. We wonder if He is ignoring us. Yet in spite of all this, we still hold on to hope and expect that it will change.

In those in-between moments, I wanted this *pray until* over, done, and through with yesterday, but God's overall plan was to bring glory out of this situation with Kaylee so there was no "immediately." God wasn't interested in our feelings or even the awkwardness of our daughter's dilemma. Kaylee had horrific separation anxiety even while I was ministering on stage. It was to the point of her being on stage with me and sitting with me until I went up to minister, even in a two-hour service. There were times when she would follow me around the altar service, holding on to my dress just to be close. I truly believe her spirit wanted to be as close to the anointing as she could get because she was comfortable there, satisfied there, and safe there. I wanted it over, but God said, "No! I'm going to use this to rub it in the devil's face as to how far I brought her, and I just need you to trust Me with your *until* prayer."

Now, the other door that Isaiah was talking about is the open door. It is, in essence, the season we want to see happen, and very quickly. At one time it was the closed door, but now it is the door that we want opened. Once we walk through that door and that season ends, we get weary and desire a new door.

For example, you are aspiring to move from an apartment to a three-bedroom home, because you need more space. In the beginning you were eager to move out of your parents' house and get your own place. You moved into a beautiful, cool apartment that you could only have imagined five years ago. But now it has been another five or six years and you are married with maybe two kids, and it has gotten a little crowded. So all you think about is, "If I could only find a house and get out of this small apartment and have room for my children to play, and have a nice area for a kitchen, and a bigger bathroom, or maybe even more than one bathroom." You forget what that first open door was like because it has become old. You've outgrown it, and it doesn't suffice anymore.

Another example is when you were young all you wanted to do was to get your driver's license, which literally meant getting your independence, and ultimately get a car. That was the quest of my two girls. They would say, "If only I could just get my license, oh, I would be so happy." We knew exactly what that meant—they wanted to be able to drive themselves around independently of me and their father.

There was a rule in our house that when you acquired your driver's license, you had to drive the gold Ford Ranger pickup truck the first year. Although it looked pretty decent, it still had some dingers on it, but it had a great radio, a CD player, and great air conditioning. But the most important thing was, it was like a tank. If anyone hit that thing, nothing and nobody was going anywhere. So the girls were happy to drive that pickup truck and hone their driving skills. Just before the year was up, they started talking about a car because the truck was getting a little old to them. So when they finally got a car, they were glad to be able to walk through that open door of getting rid of the "oldie goldie."

When I first got to college I just wanted to minister, because singleness was who I felt I was at the time. Then all of a sudden, the singleness began to sour. I found myself more and more longing for a companion and a family. For many of you reading this book, singleness has soured. There are also people who believe they are not supposed to be married to their mate anymore. The devil is a liar because God wants to restore your marriage fully! Some of you feel you are supposed to own you own business. You are tired of the waiting, and you feel you are ready to move on and get out of the in-between, beyond the tweaking, and especially beyond the pruning.

Here's what I know from experience—you can be moving out of it but still be in it. God is closing the door behind you while you are in the in-between. What is actually happening is that you can be exiting the closing door that ultimately will never open again, and that door will be your last and also your past at the same time. You will be entering into the in-between season, and at that point you are in the in-between. I have found you can't steal second base until you take your feet off of first base. You need to step out and find out, and that will always require you to get out of your comfort zone and believe God for the next.

The in-between is a place where every person who breathes and lives will experience. Many times in life, it is a place of frustration, yet on the other hand fruit is growing. Remember, patience is a fruit of the Spirit. Although it may be a small fruit or the fruit is not ripe yet, something significant is happening. "What is happening significantly?" you may ask. You are growing in the in-between and producing thirty, sixty, and a hundredfold of fruit. It is a place of development and discovery, but it feels disappointing because it's not what you thought it would be. It's true when they say it may be better on the other side of the fence, but there are still weeds on the other side of the fence that will need to be dealt with. We find ourselves looking beyond our circumstances to see what may be "over there." But the truth is, God is working on our behalf when it seems like He is doing absolutely nothing. As I stated earlier, *"All things work together for the good to them that love God, to them who are the called according to his purpose"* (Rom. 8:28).

Here's the good news—everybody's in-between is different; no one has the same in-between. How soon doors begin to open is based entirely on readiness, maturity, and understanding.

Jamie and I have found in our in-between seasons that our obedience level becomes intense. We have learned to sow more seed, and not just financially. We sow in tears, in worship, in fasting, and we sow relationally in prayer. What does that mean? It means that there is simple agreement between two parties believing and calling forth those things which are not as though they are. This season is also a place where there are no angels, no singers, dancers, or B3 organs playing in the background. You don't necessarily hear the wind blowing in the mulberry trees, and there are not many epiphany moments in the in-between season. It is a simple trust in God being God in your life and Him bringing you to a place of abandonment and even an uncomfortable trust. Isaiah 46:8-10 says this:

> *Remember this, and show yourselves men; recall to mind, O you transgressors. Remember the former things of old, for I am God, and there is no other; I am God, and there is none like Me, declaring the end from the beginning, and from ancient times things that are not yet done, saying, "My counsel shall stand, and I will do all my pleasure" (NKJV).*

In that scripture alone, God describes Himself as declaring your ending from your beginning. He is calling your ending from a place that already exists and bringing or delivering it to you where you exist now. Jesus prayed this by saying, *"Your kingdom come. Your will be done, on earth as it is in heaven"* (Matt. 6:10 NKJV). He was calling forth things that were foreordained in the heavens to be actualized in the now in our human experience. Job said you will decree a thing and it will be established (see Job 22:28).

What you decree is not current. Actually, what you decree is something you see, and then through prayer and fasting God brings it to you in the supernatural. This is God's promise to you between the closed door and the open door, which is the positon of being in-between. It is not rejection, though the enemy would have us think that God has rejected us or He has refused our requests or destroyed our dream. Satan will tell you that God has taken your ability to anticipate in faith and denied you and said, "*No, that is not My will for your life.*" The truth of the matter is, it is the process of God that gets us to the promise, and too often we don't want to go through the process.

My husband describes growing up and going on small business trips with his dad to tune pianos at people's homes and churches and concert halls. Oftentimes, they would see trains in some of the small towns they would go through. He recalls how his dad would pull up to a train track while a passing train was going by, and to keep boredom at a minimum he would challenge him and his brothers to try and count the cars as the train was passing them. You can imagine the turning of the little heads as they were trying to count the moving cars of a train. It is literally impossible, but it sure made up for having to pacify little ones.

When a train is passing, it feels like nothing is going on; you're just sitting there and something else is going by you so fast, like time—hours, days, and life itself. You feel as if things are going by so fast and everybody else is getting blessed; everybody else is increasing; everybody else is getting married, getting a job, and getting a house; and everybody else's dreams are coming true, and yet you are sitting at the train track counting cars.

But that is the in-between. It's still a part of the train; it's not the engine; it's not the caboose, but it is what ties the two ends together. Those cars are just as important as the engine and the caboose. Likewise, your in-between moment ties your last season with your coming season. Sometimes, the in-between is tough and challenging to your faith, but like Isaac we sow in seasons of drought and rain.

A perfect example of a season of challenge is when my husband had graduated from college and he got a job at a trucking company. He worked there for a while, but the job really wasn't what he wanted to do, obviously, so he waited and prayed. One day he got a call that a door had opened for him to move to Cleveland, Tennessee and play music, which was his dream. He was so pumped at the possibility, so off to Cleveland he went. He got his last paycheck after he had already moved to Cleveland.

To his surprise, his former boss left a phone message accusing him of wasting the company's time and falling asleep on the job. He was really upset and angry because Jamie had left his company to go and pursue his dream. The devil hates it when you get promoted. As I mentioned earlier, Isaac sowed in the land of famine, and in the same year he reaped a hundredfold. The Bible says that Isaac became so prosperous that his enemies hated him. Well, I guess this enemy was upset because Jamie had found favor.

So his last paycheck came through the mail straight to the apartment where he lived. Well, instead of taking the much-needed check and going to cash it, Jamie turned right around and sent it back with a "return to sender" on it. He told his former boss, "I regret the way you feel; however, everything you said about me is not true. I want you to know that I love where I am right now and

I know this is where God would have me be. Since you accused me of doing wrong to your company, I am sowing this check back to you for you to put it back into your company." He never heard back from this man or the company, but he had a resolve and a peace of mind that the enemy couldn't take from him.

Sometimes you have to sow a seed into your season of adversity to announce to God and all of hell how thankful you are for the past season. The enemy thought he had him, but when Jamie sowed into his destiny and purpose it defeated the enemy's lie. In that season he was able to purchase a car that he desperately needed. Sometimes you have to be so determined that hell will not get the last word about what God has promised to you. That check was $120 but he was determined to sow into his season of adversity.

Some of you need to heed this word and start to sow into your season of misery, adversity, and challenge and start enjoying the provision of the promise. Sometimes the key to an open door is sowing into the last season where you thought you were being rejected and defeated.

Here's the reality of it. To sow into what you call misery or adversity is actually sowing into what God used to make a difference in your life. The last door was not necessarily the devil, but an opportunity to sow into your history. The last door is just as much God's will as the door that's about to open up to you. So when you honor God with what He did in the last season, it gives Him an opportunity to catapult you to your next.

When I first started itinerant ministry, I used to take the tithe of the honorarium that was given to me from any church—no matter what it was, large or small—and send it back to that church with a thank you to the pastor. I would take the opportunity to say, "I want to thank you for allowing me to be in your church this weekend and minister to your congregation, and I want to tithe back into what you are doing in that city." What I am living in right now is the result of the gifts and giving that we gave because we were believing for open doors. Our prayer was, *"Lord, if You will just open doors for us, we will go wherever You take us. It doesn't matter the size; I want to be used by You."*

So, the closing of a door or a season is not negative; it is the ending of one season and the beginning of a new one. If you honored God in your last season, He can trust you with the next. He didn't forget our $20 off the $200 honorarium. Oh, I know it wasn't much, but today we are living out the blessings of those seeds in more ways than one.

I remember there were times when pastors would call my husband and say, "Hey listen, Brother Tuttle, I just got a check today from you and your wife, can you tell me what this is for?"

Jamie would then explain, "Well sir, we just typically give a tithe back into the church and the pastors who blessed us. I hope you will receive it as a seed to bless your church back." God doesn't miss things like that; He notices those small things. Jesus took notice of the widow woman, even though what she gave was less than a penny. He explained to His disciples, *"this poor widow hath cast in more than they all"* (Luke 21:3).

I remember traveling with the recruitment group from the university where I met my husband. As soon as we got back into town, the students scurried off to class, but because I had already graduated I would stay behind to get the bus cleaned and ready for the next trip. I would scrub the toilet, vacuum the floors, and take all the sheets off the bunks and take them to my house and get them laundered and then put back in place. Little did I know that because I was faithful over someone else's bus, to keep it clean and nice, sometime later God gave us our own bus.

Sometimes the in-between will come up on you and be disguised and you never know what God has planned, but He is checking your integrity meter to see if you will be faithful over the little so that He can bless you with the big. In the season of *pray until*, you must respect the in-between. You must respect the now season, because it is all a part of the formula of the Kingdom of God and it will catapult you to the next.

What's the formula? Seeking. Praying. Believing. Dedication. Time. Faithfulness. Godly character. Godly integrity. One of the things you will come to know is that God is a God who will change the times and the seasons in order to fulfill His promise. If He made the sun stand still; if He parted the Red Sea; if He turned the water into wine; if He raised Lazarus and a thousand other things our Bible tells us He did, He will surely come to our aid and rescue.

Remember, He changes the times and the seasons, but He doesn't change His formula. Matthew 6:33 says, "*But seek ye first the kingdom of God, and his righteousness; and all these things shall be added unto you.*" The same formula has worked through every season since the very beginning. It's not the changing of the formula; it's the changing of the season. It's not a change of how you do it, but when you do it. God says He changes not, which means whatever He has put in place has always worked.

You sow in times of famine; you sow in times of emptiness; you sow in times of desperation, and you sow in times of joy. You sow everything from prayer to money; you sow tears to treasure. You sow everything about you. You sow into the hard times so that the fruit comes in the best times and the worst times. Just keep in mind, the formula never changes. Seek first the Kingdom of God and His righteousness, and everything about Him, everything about His domain, everything about His abode, everything about His Word, about who He is, His character, and His attributes will be added to you. We sow into what His name is to us and what He means to us.

The Bible says that when you seek Him in this manner then all these things will be added to you. What I have found out is that all means all. There is not one thing on the "all" menu that surprises God, because He already knows in His infinite omniscience what you need and want.

I love the fact that He already knows what you're going to put on paper, or what you have in your heart, because He already understands the all. Your *all* will never surprise God; it will never catch Him off-guard; it never shakes or quakes Him. Here's the great news—your *all* is as special to Him as His *all* is to you. Just as special as the sun rising and setting, the earth moving on its axis, and the rainbow in the sky—that's how special your *all* is to Him.

He reminds us that all these things shall be added to us. It is His formula, and His formula is His covenant. One thing that God cannot do is fail, which means His covenant doesn't fail. Our Father never walks away from His covenant over our lives. He never forgets it; He never despises it, and He will hold to His covenant to the very end, and nobody can stop what God is about to do in your life.

In the old door and old season, His covenant still stands true. His covenant is more real than ever before, and in your next season His covenant will prove faithful and long-suffering to the very end of the world. It will continue longer than any of His creation will continue. His Word and His promises to you will not be shaken or ever fade away—that's the promise of the in-between. He will prove Himself faithful right where you are in the reality of life. You just have to hold on to hope!

Your *Pray Until* Challenge

- As you are in your in-between, can you still pray, "Lord, not my will but Your will be done"?

- Can you think of a time when God closed a door and you seemed to have lost your way?

- Did you wait for the next door to open?

- Remember, delay is not denial. Hold on to what God said in the light when you are in the dark, moving from one doorway to another.

Chapter 10

REAL PERSON, REAL WORLD, REAL GOD

This is what I have asked of God for you: that you will be encouraged and knit together by strong ties of love, and that you will have the rich experience of knowing Christ with real certainty and clear understanding.

—COLOSSIANS 2:2 TLB

Lord, sustain me as you promised, that I may live! Do not let my hope be crushed.

—PSALM 119:116 NLT

Such hope [in God's promises] never disappoints us, because God's love has been abundantly poured out within our hearts through the Holy Spirit who was given to us.

—ROMANS 5:5 AMP

A day without prayer is a day without blessing, and a life without prayer is a life without power.

—EDWIN HARVEY

Once all the villagers decided to pray for rain. On the day of prayer, all the people gathered, but only one boy came with an umbrella. That is faith!

When you throw babies in the air, they laugh because they know you will catch them. That is trust!

Every single night we go to bed without any assurance of being alive the next morning, but still we set alarms to wake up. That is hope!

We plan big things for tomorrow in spite of zero knowledge of the future. That is confidence!

We see the world suffering, but still we get married and have children. That is love!

On an old man's shirt was written a sentence: "I am not 80 years old; I am sweet 16 with 64 years of experience." That is attitude!

—UNKNOWN

I love these different sayings because they tell you life is real. And in this life you have a choice to see the glass half empty or half full; it's your attitude that determines it. Someone has said that *life happens!* And it does! Look at these real-life examples:

- You wake up in the morning and discover some gray hairs on your head and you realize that you are getting older.

- You wake up on the other side of the bed feeling a bit off-kilter.

- Bills, bills, bills.

- There are disagreements with your spouse and your children.

- Separation and then divorce happens.

- Debt accumulates.

- Bankruptcy looks inevitable.

- Sickness comes.

- A pandemic that affects the whole world takes place.

- Death occurs.

All of these things are a part of "Life." And believe me when I tell you, life definitely will come at you. That is *real life* in a *real world* around *real people.* Here is the good news though—*God is also real and there is hope in the midst of all of life!*

Experience, just like life, is a hard teacher, because it gives the test first and then the lesson afterward. Because of that, when you are pursuing your *until* prayers, you have to maintain *hope.* You must be shockproof, sober, mature, levelheaded, but at the same time lighthearted, with childlike faith. What is the secret to receiving your miracle and maintaining hope in the midst of this real-life world?

Holding on to hope!

What is hope? Hope is to have confidence, trust, desire, and to consider that with God all things are possible!

My favorite definition is "the longing and desire for something accompanied by the belief in the possibility of its occurrence." First Peter 1:3 talks about the living hope:

Praise be to the God and Father of our Lord Jesus Christ! In his great mercy he has given us new birth into a living hope through the resurrection of Jesus Christ from the dead (NIV).

It's interesting that a *living hope* is accompanied by a *resurrection*. It really is a paradox. Why would you need a living hope to be accompanied by a resurrection? Where is the death in this situation? That is the whole point of death—in order for there to be a resurrection, there has to be a death in the equation somewhere. But that is the glorious truth—there was a death, Jesus experienced that death, but because God raised Him from the dead we now have a living hope in the person of Jesus. Because of that hope, Jesus gives us a promise that our hope is living, active, and producing.

David said, *"My hope is in You"* (Ps. 39:7 NKJV). Lamentations 3:26 declares, *"It is good to both hope and wait quietly for the salvation of the Lord"* (TLB). Psalm 119:147: *"I hope in Your word"* (NKJV). Proverbs 23:18: *"Your hope will not be cut off"* (NKJV). Consider the last verse in the love chapter, First Corinthians 13: *"And now these three remain: faith, hope and love. But the greatest of these is love"* (1 Cor. 13:13 NIV).

There is an emphasis on these powerful words, but Paul tells us what will last forever, and here is the reason why. When it is all said and done, we will not need faith in Heaven because our *faith* will have come into sight!

We will not need hope, because our *hope* will be realized—there will be no more reason to hope to go to Heaven and to be with Jesus forever because we will be with Him!

So the only thing that will last forever will be *love,* and God is love. Therefore, love will last throughout the eternities of the eternities!

This beautiful word, *hope,* is a confidence that endures in the middle of chaos; it is a joy when tears should be the norm. During my *pray until* moments I discovered that hope in God will sustain you! It gets you through another day and then another day with a spring in your step.

Romans 12:12 admonishes you to "Be joyful in hope" (NIV). Paul prayed this over us in Romans 15:13: *"May the God of hope fill you with all joy and peace as you trust in him, so that you may over-flow with hope by the power of the Holy Spirit"* (NIV).

We need to be hope carriers for the people around us and for the household of faith, because the greater one lives in us. Every-where people are looking for someone who *acts like* they know where they are going. Your faith will definitely be tried as you trust in the unseen hand of your Father, but it will definitely not be shaken. God is giving you an unshakable resolve to see this thing to the end!

You may get to a point as Jamie and I did at times and feel as Jeremiah felt:

> *You have moved my soul far from peace; I have forgot-ten prosperity. And I said, "My strength and my hope have perished from the Lord"* (Lamentations 3:17-18 NKJV).

These emotions are very real as you are facing your *pray until* times, but the next verses tell the whole story:

> *Remember my affliction and roaming, the wormwood and the gall. My soul still remembers and sinks within me. This I recall to my mind, therefore I have hope. Through the Lord's mercies we are not consumed, because His compassions fail not. They are new every morning;*

great is Your faithfulness. "The Lord is my portion," *says, my soul, "therefore I hope in Him"* (Lamentations 3:19-24 NKJV).

Take to heart that He is your portion. No matter how many things may skyrocket toward us every day, we must remember that God is our portion and He is all we need. When we look at the situation, we take courage knowing:

For He shall give His angels charge over you, to keep you *in all your ways. In their hands they shall bear you up,* *lest you dash your foot against a stone* (Psalm 91:11-12 NKJV).

Even though this world we are living in is fallen, diseased, and full of trouble and heartache, it makes us long for Heaven all the more. We live in the world as the villagers in the story above lived it. We live it in *faith, hope, confidence, trust, and with an attitude of gratitude.*

One of my greatest moments of hope came in a green room when a beautiful woman who was serving guests walked over to me and slipped me a note. The note was a very simple page from a pretty little notepad. Simply put, the note said, "God says to tell you, 'Not much longer.' I don't know what that means, Sister Judy, but I hope that encourages you." Oh, I couldn't get to the bathroom fast enough to release the streams of tears coming down my face. Only God in Heaven knows the hope that little note brought me. By the way, I still have that note.

During that time, Jamie and I didn't often share what we were going through, both to protect Kaylee and to keep on a path of focused prayer without a lot of voices in our ears. However, there was one friend that I could turn to. Karen Wheaton and I have been close friends for the past 30 years. But she is more than a friend, she is a true sister, comrade, and warrior partner. Karen hosts an event called Kids Ramp every summer in Hamilton, Alabama. While still in the middle of our battle, Jamie and I decided it would be a great thing to take Kaylee and Erica to Kids Ramp. It was a "God moment." It was God's moment and God's timing to put Kaylee on a trajectory toward her deliverance. During that Kids Ramp, Kaylee was gloriously baptized in the Holy Spirit with the evidence of speaking in tongues. I can confidently say that was the turning point to things beginning to shift and change. Thank God for a woman that has said "yes" to empowering this generation. In a time of wondering, *How much longer? Does He really know what we're going through?* The answer to that is, "Yes, a million times yes!" He knows what you are facing, and at just the right time it will all turn for your good.

There is a saying that my husband and I use often when we greet our friends. We ask them the question, "All is well?" meaning, how is your life, your family, your church, and everything that has to do with you? We're not just casually asking to make conversation; we really want to know the real facts about our friends. One thing is for sure, there is no pretending about life. When things are not well, we declare to each other a faith declaration, "All shall be well!"

Sometimes when they deem it necessary, they will respond to us, "We choose to believe the report of the Lord. So all is well."

That reminds me of the story of the Shunammite's son in Second Kings 4. This woman and her husband were people of means. They even built an extra room on their home for the prophet Elisha. One day Elisha asked his servant what he could do for her. The servant replied, *"She has no son, and her husband is old"* (2 Kings 4:14 NKJV).

So Elisha said to her, *"About this time next year you shall embrace a son"* (2 Kings 4:16 NKJV).

So at the appointed time she did, in fact, have a son. One day while the boy was with his father, scholars believe he had a sunstroke, and in his mother's arms he died. The mother put the child on Elisha's bed and shut the door. You can imagine a mother knowing her promised child is now dead, and yet with determination she is boldly in hot pursuit of the man who gave her the prophecy about the child.

When the prophet saw her coming in the distance, he sent his servant, Gehazi, asking, *"Is it well with you?"* She answered, *"It is well"* (2 Kings 4:26 NKJV). At this point I don't know if the woman was speaking from her faith, or she was patronizing the servant of Elisha because she didn't want to talk to him—she wanted to speak to the *real* man of God. When she came near to Elisha, in desperation she grabbed hold of his feet to say, in essence, "I've got something to say to you and you're going to listen and not go anywhere." She started to pepper him with questions of the real world.

> *Did I desire a son of my lord? did I not say, Do not deceive me?* (2 Kings 4:28)

Further back in the chapter, when the prophet Elisha began to prophesy a son, the woman even said to him:

> *"No, my lord!" she cried. "O man of God, don't deceive me and get my hopes up like that"* (2 Kings 4:16 NLT).

Sometimes, we sink so much in despair that we don't even want to hear a prophetic word spoken to us, for fear that our hopes will be dashed to pieces. This woman had probably hoped against hope many times, believing that she would have a child. Then here came this man of God who began to prophesy her dream. I want to encourage you to always be willing to hear the Word of the Lord from a powerful man or woman of God. Our hope should not necessarily be in the one giving the message; rather, our hope should be in the Word spoken and confirmed in our hearts by the speaking of the Spirit of God in the secret place.

After all that had happened, she made her way to the prophet and grabbed hold of him. From the outside looking in, it seems Elisha wanted to go the easy route and send his servant, Gehazi, with Elisha's staff, but the woman replied, *"As the Lord lives, and as your soul lives, I will not leave you"* (2 Kings 4:30 NKJV). In essence she said, "I have come this far raising this boy, believing your words, and now here I am with a promised child who is dead! I need a miracle!" This woman believed the same God who heard the man of God's prayer the first time was going to hear him again, and she was right!

In other words, she was saying, "You're going to go back with me and lay your hands on this child and I'm going to get my miracle." Sometimes you have to remind God of what *He said.*

The next verse says, *"So he arose and followed her"* (2 Kings 4:30 NKJV). When he entered the room, the boy was lying dead on Elisha's bed, and he went and laid his body on the child two times, and the body of the boy began to be warm—meaning his body was already cold and lifeless. Then by a divine miracle, he sneezed seven times and opened his eyes. He was alive, and at the end *all was well!*

That tells me we must be relentless in our *until* prayer. Don't let people, passiveness, and real things keep you from a real God, because at any given minute, anything can happen with God! You need to prophesy in this season, "Things are starting to warm up! Oh, I haven't heard any sneezes yet, but there is about to be a burst of life."

God never said you would not have times of despair, seeming hopelessness, trouble, and problems. As a matter of fact, He promised them. Jesus said, *"In this world you will have trouble. But take heart! I have overcome the world!"* (John 16:33 NIV).

There will be days of uncertainty, just like John the Baptist when he told his disciples to go and ask Jesus, *"Are you the one who is to come, or should we expect someone else?"* (Matt. 11:3 NIV). That was very real! Jesus told John's disciples:

> *Go back and report to John what you hear and see: The blind receive sight, the lame walk, those who have leprosy are cleansed, the deaf hear, the dead are raised, and the good news is proclaimed to the poor. Blessed is anyone who does not stumble on account of me* (Matthew 11:4-6 NIV).

John knew that he was in deep trouble, and he just wanted the assurance that he was still on the right track. Let me just take this opportunity to tell you, all of hell may be assailing you and your marriage right now, but you're still on the right track. Your son or daughter may have walked in your house with some of the most disturbing news, but you're still on the right track. You may not have two nickels to rub together, but you're still on the right track. God has already tracked your comeback from a setback, and the enemy is going to wish he would have never touched you and your life. God knows all and hears all, and He is still sitting enthroned in the heavens. As a child of God, you have a direct line into Heaven's courts through the blood of Jesus and you also have access to approach the throne of God with holy boldness and make your requests known to Christ (see Phil. 4:6). And His promise is that He will hear from Heaven!

It seems we live in a day and hour when you don't know the difference between what is real or unreal. We hear about everything being fake, and in many cases that is true. I look back even at my age and see how far technology has come and it is really dizzying. I'm reminded of the scripture in Daniel 12:4:

> *But thou, O Daniel, shut up the words, and seal the book, even to the time of the end: many shall run to and fro, and knowledge shall be increased.*

Technology and AI are the fastest growing phenomena of our day. Quite honestly, it is unbelievable how fast things are changing. In the real world:

- Sometimes our loved one dies after we pray and believe for a miracle.
- Sometimes God's people get into accidents that really don't make sense.
- Children come home and announce things that are life-altering.
- We are overlooked for a job promotion.
- We lose our jobs.
- We experience sickness and disease in our bodies.

Yes, bad things happen to good people in a real world. But we must still continue to love, laugh, speak life, pray and believe, and never stop believing for a supernatural intervention.

For our light affliction, which is but for a moment, worketh for us a far more exceeding and eternal weight of glory (2 Corinthians 4:17).

Something is working that makes the enemy's skin crawl—his time is almost up! We are in the fight of our lives. Something is happening like we have never seen before. In the midst of all of hell there is a shifting in the atmosphere—something is moving and changing. What will the future be like for our children and our grandchildren?

In this culture, relativism is completely trying to take over our everyday lives and affairs. The independent spirit says, "I will let my flesh dictate to me what feels good or not. Right or wrong depends entirely on what I believe and the circumstances that I find myself in at the present moment of time." It seems people have been deceived by a prevailing lie that there is no absolute truth. What is absolute truth? Absolute truth is an unalterable fact. Here are some absolute truths:

- If you jump off the roof of a ten-story building, you will fall to the ground.

- If an airplane just happens to run out of fuel 30,000 feet in the air, it will absolutely fall.

- If you stick your hand in a raging fire, you will be burned.

On and on we could go from there, but let it suffice to say there are absolutes! Here are just a few of my strongest absolutes, taken from the song "Statement of Faith":

- I believe Jesus is the Holy Son of God!

- He came to earth and lived a perfect and spotless life.

- I believe He bled and died on a cruel cross and Jesus made the greatest sacrifice!

- I believe He rose again and that He lives today.

- I believe He's coming back for us.

- I believe the Bible is the Word of God given to the world to show the way.

- I believe in loyalty to God and commitment to the church.

- I believe in the priority of the family.

- I believe in the sanctity of marriage.

- I believe Jesus is coming again!

Those, my friend, are some of my absolutes!

In everyday life, we are in a battle for the family—we are in a battle for the very core and soul of our nation. People are dealing with confusion, anger, frustration, stress, anxiety, and depression. They are talking about suicide more than ever, and the sad truth is that many of these people are our kids. Hopelessness has risen in the hearts of our children.

We are also in a battle for our religious freedom in the church, where the right to even exist is being questioned. There is a war that is going on with our fathers. They are missing in the family unit.

When life seems to spiral out of control, people begin to wonder, "What is really happening?" The last two years have created a feeling of being beat up, and people are feeling very fragile and weak. It seems everything that was normal has suddenly disappeared. But there is hope for our country and our families.

Hope gives you the strength to not give up and to outlast the unbearable. In other words, you can't quit! You hear the voice of God say, "I heard your prayer—trust my timing." Why? Because at any given minute or moment, God can shift you from waiting on it to walking in it!

Paul was confronted with a very strange and dynamic dilemma in Acts 27. It is the story of Paul being on the ship as a prisoner being taken to Rome. Dr. Shirley Arnold has a great perspective on Paul's dilemma—he had to get on that ship, yet the ship was not his choice. He even told them, "Do not set sail." But the Bible says that they talked amongst themselves—in other words, the experts got together—and decided that Paul didn't know what he was talking about.

Then they met up with a storm. The storm was not his choice!

The people were not his choice!

Then look what happened. It got so bad that literally it looked like everything was going to be lost and destroyed, and the Bible goes so far as to say there was no hope!

> *Now when neither sun nor stars appeared for many days, and no small tempest beat on us* [implying that it was a very big tempest], *all hope that we would be saved was finally given up* (Acts 27:20 NKJV).

But because of who he was, Paul was clearly aware that, yes, everything would probably be lost—except for one thing. He was on the ship!

That's right, Paul was on the ship.

Jesus was on the boat (see Matt. 8).

There's a fourth man in the fire (see Dan. 3), and *those who are with us are more than those who are with them*" (2 Kings 6:16 NKJV).

That's what has to be engrafted in your mind: "I am on this ship, the Captain of this ship is Jesus, and as long as I am on this thing, it's not going down!" Your family needs to see your resolve. Your husband needs to see your determination. Your wife needs to understand you are not a quitter. Out of all the strong points in your life, hope is your forte!

Then the voice of God began to speak. When you are in a storm you have to listen *to* and *for* the divine voice of God. God said, "Listen, nobody is going to die."

Paul's presence sanctified the storm, the ship, and the people. Your presence in the midst of this storm is so intimidating because Jesus is at the helm and you shall not be moved. There is no room for error as long as you are trusting in His strong arms to carry you through.

Then they came to a place where the captain of the ship put a boat down in the water pretending to check the depth, but they were planning an escape. But Paul told them all, "If you jump ship, there are no guarantees you will be saved." Let me tell you, you have no choice but to remain faithful to the instructions given. Stay put! Continue to meditate on God's Word! Plead the blood!

Continually speak the name of Jesus over the situation and pray and make your confession of faith daily! When Paul gave them the final warning, they began to destroy every escape route.

This is a season when you will have to destroy everything that will hinder you from getting to the other side. Everything that is not a direct instruction from the Holy Spirit must be destroyed.

We can't lose hope; we can't jump ship. We are going to the other side. There is a next! You will come through this stronger, not weaker. You can't forget that God is for us! You can't jump! He's coming with power and hope, and now is the time for miracles.

When you are contending for your *until* prayers, you need someone in your face who will be bold enough to speak and provoke you to recognize that the very next breath you take could be your breakthrough. You never know the threshold where your miracle will be manifested. I love the song I sing sometimes, "You're one step away from your miracle." Here's the rub about that—if you give up, your next step could have been exactly what you have been waiting for. Don't give up; instead, pursue, overtake, and recover all...but especially practice staying in His peace.

Your *Pray Until* Challenge

- Ask God to instill godly wisdom and discernment as you move through this season of believing for an *until* prayer to be answered as you are looking at the hard facts.

- Are you prone to melt down or to kneel down in prayer?

- In dire situations do you fast and pray?

- Have you jumped ship over the past two to three years? If so, isn't it time to get back on the boat?

Chapter 11

Stay in Peace by Practicing the Presence—Until!

You will guard him and keep him in perfect and constant peace whose mind [both its inclination and its character] is stayed on You, because he commits himself to You, leans on You, and hopes confidently in You.

—Isaiah 26:3 AMPC

An unpeaceful mind cannot operate normally. Hence the Apostle teaches us to *"have no anxiety about anything"* (Phil. 4:6). Deliver all anxious thoughts to God as soon as they arise. Let the peace of God maintain your heart and mind.

—Watchman Nee[1]

No man is greater than his prayer life.

—Leonard Ravenhill

There is a secret to maintaining your peace stance, and that is intentionally focusing on keeping your heart and mind centered on staying in a place of safety with His presence. The enemy is always trying to chase you away from the presence of God, because he understands that real peace will be found in His presence. Peace is not the absence of problems but the presence of Jesus in the midst of them.

In his devotional *Sparkling Gems from the Greek II*, Rick Renner describes a very interesting word. He uses the scripture, *"For the Son of man is come to seek and to save that which was lost"* (Luke 19:10).

> It tells us that Jesus has put forth and is putting forth His best efforts to actively seek to save and restore whatever Satan has tried to steal, kill, or destroy. What does "save" mean in this case? It is translated from the Greek word sodzo, which mainly implies rescue, such as rescue from a raging sea, rescue from an illness, rescue from immediate danger, and so forth. Inherent in this type of "rescue" is one's return to safety and soundness. ...Jesus wants to rescue and return us to a state of normalcy, safety, and recovery...a fully restorative operation.[2]

This is a time to confront some things that you are dealing with and things that need to be resolved in your will, your mind, and your emotions. The word *sodzo* also carries the idea of being "safe and sound, healed, delivered, made whole, and rest."

Sodzo ministry is used many times in the New Testament, and it is a ministry that God has used to help people come to terms with things they are dealing with in their hearts and minds. In Matthew 11:28, Jesus gives a special invitation for His children to come and rest: *"Come to me, all you who are weary and burdened, and I will give you rest"* (NIV).

The Greek word for *rest* in Jesus' invitation is an encouraging word. It means "to permit a person to stop moving in order to seek refreshment or to regain strength" (Rick Renner, *Sparkling Gems*). The invitation is, "Come to Me." Your peace is a huge gift that God has given to all His children. Jesus said:

> *I am leaving you with a gift—peace of mind and heart.*
> *And the peace I give is a gift the world cannot give. So*
> *don't be troubled or afraid* (John 14:27 NLT).

Someone has said, "Anything that costs you your peace is too expensive." As a matter of fact, Paul said, "*If it is possible, as far as it depends on you, live at peace with everyone*" (Rom. 12:18 NIV).

Wow! That seems a little lofty in the natural, but that is an admonition from Paul to give us an instruction in how to live your life in peace. I'm glad that he said, "If at all possible," meaning sometimes it is not possible. At some point in your life you will encounter people who are determined to *not* live in peace and to make everyone else's life as miserable as theirs. But God wants everyone to live in peace. I believe if we practice peace, then it will shine a light on others to desire that same peace. We have a responsibility to the "if at all possible" admonition, though. So let me be quick to say, if there are things in your life that you wouldn't want to come to light, then they must be renounced. Anything between your soul and your Savior needs to be dealt with immediately.

Personally, I remember as a child growing up in church that the last thing said before the dismissal prayer was, "Are all hearts and minds clear?" The pastor in those days was concerned if anyone had anything to add to what had already been said. If anyone had any issues that needed prayer that week, he would allow for those things to be spoken out.

It's very simple to do in theory, but we must make a decisive choice to say, "I'm getting that out of my heart. I will not allow that to remain fixed in my mind. Instead, I will renounce it and move on with my assignment."

The Adamic nature is always in constant battle with the things of the spirit. That is why you have to guard your heart and daily put on the breastplate of righteousness. Paul gives a caution to the church in Corinth, saying:

> *Therefore seeing we have this ministry, as we have received mercy, we faint not; but have renounced the hidden things of dishonesty, not walking in craftiness, nor handling the word of God deceitfully; but by manifestation of the truth commending ourselves to every man's conscience in the sight of God* (2 Corinthians 4:1-2).

The Bible very plainly calls it *walking in craftiness* or, "being underhanded, devising evil schemes, being cunning or being deceitful." As people of God, our standard is the Word of God. Our standard is to lift up righteousness and holiness in the fear and the admonition of the Lord.

When pursuing your *until* prayer, you will never experience peace unless certain heart issues are resolved. Proverbs says, "*Guard your heart above all else, for it determines the course of your life*" (Prov. 4:23 NLT). What I have found is that the peace of God will wash away my worry, which comes to take up all my precious time and energy. The psalmist said, *"Be still, and know that I am God"* (Ps. 46:10).

I think it is interesting that the original Hebrew root of *be still* doesn't mean to be quiet; it means "let go." So in actuality he is saying, "Let go and let God," and when you do, you will understand fully the joy of knowing real peace.

Jesus said, *"My sheep hear my voice, and I know them, and they follow me"* (John 10:27), and in John 10:5 he says, *"And a stranger will they not follow."* We know how the enemy comes at us to trick, scheme, and control the narrative in our lives. That's when we have to HALT, and examine the things around us or we will fall for his lies quickly. When you are:

- Hungry
- Angry
- Lonely
- Tired

Wisdom would say, never make a major decision, or speak out, or make up your mind about anything when you are feeling any of these emotions. You need to HALT! Stop! Those are the worst times to do anything. God just wants you to stay in His peace and leave the rest to Him.

Paul exhorts us to never give in to the schemes of the enemy because we are not ignorant concerning the devices of the devil (see 2 Cor. 2:11). Look at the contrast between the enemy's voice and God's voice:

God's Voice	Satan's Voice
stills you	rushes you
leads you	pushes you
reassures you	frightens you
enlightens you	confuses you
encourages you	discourages you
comforts you	worries you
calms you	obsesses you
convicts you	condemns you

The psalmist says, "*I will both lay me down in peace, and sleep: for thou, Lord, only makest me dwell in safety*" (Ps. 4:8).

God is a God of love and order. If the voice you are hearing doesn't sound like those things, then it is not from Him. Conflict and worry stem from a place of fear, and Paul says, "*God is not the author of confusion, but of peace*" (1 Cor. 14:33). Now if God is not the author of confusion, my question becomes, "Who is?" The enemy always has strategies to use against us to derail our peace. He always wants to use fear, doubt, and unbelief, because these are the enemies of your faith.

- Fear says, "I am afraid that it won't happen."
- Doubt says, "I honestly doubt that anything will come of this."
- Unbelief echoes, "No, it will never happen."

But don't forget, "*He is a liar and the father of lies*" (John 8:44 NIV). The devil comes to you to tell you that all these things you have been reading about in this book and especially the Bible are not working and never will work. That's when you have to get really excited, because in reality the opposite is the truth. He is just lying to you again.

Have you ever considered the word *fear?* There are many acronyms for it; here are two:

Forget		**F**ace
Everything	OR	**E**verything
And		**A**nd
Run		**R**ise

One thing about the people of God is that we don't have to run and hide from anything. Proverbs 28:1 says, *"The wicked flee when no man pursueth: but the righteous are bold as a lion."*

You can be bold toward your situation and have confidence because of your God. Daniel 11:32 declares, *"But the people who know their God shall be strong, and carry out great exploits"* (NKJV). We can carry out great and mighty exploits because of the greatness of our God and all of His promises. The Bible promises rest to the people of God in Hebrews 4:9: *"There remains, then, a Sabbath-rest for the people of God"* (NIV).

The Bible says in Psalm 92:10, *"But my horn You have exalted like a wild ox; I have been anointed with fresh oil"* (NKJV). When the enemy comes with his claws upon us, he will slip because of the oil of the anointing of the Holy Spirit that God has deposited on us. This is the time to seek the filling of the Holy Spirit and always have that fresh oil activated in us.

167

The enemy wants to sabotage our minds and steal our peace. But remember that peace is one of the nine fruits of being a child of God. With the oily anointing upon us, we can shift the enemy's plans and make him utterly fall in his own steps.

Many times in my life I have had to deliberately wrap myself up in my prayer tallit and receive the peace of God in my heart for a certain season that I was walking through. When I would be totally wrapped up in my prayer shawl, there would come wonderful times of great comfort, peace, and a real sense of contentment from the Holy Spirit.

God spoke through Isaiah, saying:

> *For thus says the Lord God, the Holy One of Israel: "In returning and rest you shall be saved; in quietness and confidence shall be your strength"* (Isaiah 30:15 NKJV).

I love how Zephaniah says it:

> *The Lord thy God in the midst of thee is mighty; he will save, he will rejoice over thee with joy; he will rest in his love, he will joy over thee with singing* (Zephaniah 3:17).

Here is what God showed me. It's like a platoon, because we are all God's soldiers in His army, marching with a certain beat from Heaven. But we are marching to a different drummer—the Holy Spirit, the Spirit of God, the Spirit of Peace. We are warriors and our Lord is the Captain of the host of Heaven's armies. One of the things that will bring peace is to know you are not alone as you walk out this journey.

First of all, we know that the victory is already won. Second, we have the Father, Son, and Holy Spirit with us, so we are not alone.

Then, never forget that there is a whole cloud of witnesses and angels that surround the people of God day and night.

The story of Elisha and his servant is a prime example of us never being alone. The king of Aram was so upset with Elisha for always telling the king of Israel the secret plans that he was making to destroy God's people. He thought that some of his people were actually sabotaging him and telling the warfare secrets, but God was the one in the center of it all. Word of caution—never, ever fight against God!

One day, the king of Aram sent his troops with horses and chariots to surround the place where Elijah and his servant were and to seize him at Dothan. The story continues:

> *So one night the king of Aram sent a great army with many chariots and horses to surround the city.*
>
> *When the servant of the man of God got up early the next morning and went outside, there were troops, horses, and chariots everywhere. "Oh, sir, what will we do now?" the young man cried to Elisha.*
>
> *"Don't be afraid!" Elisha told him. "For there are more on our side than on theirs!" Then Elisha prayed, "O Lord, open his eyes and let him see!" The Lord opened the young man's eyes, and when he looked up, he saw that the hillside around Elisha was filled with horses and chariots of fire* (2 Kings 6:14-17 NLT).

Oh hallelujah! That is so exciting to me to know that there are more on my side than the enemy's side! Notice what kind of chariots and horses there were—they were supernatural horses and chariots of fire. When all of hell is assailing you, just look up! You will see your enemy is always outnumbered!

One of the things I had to learn to do during our crisis with Kaylee was to keep my head high, looking for the promise to show up at any moment. I knew it was on the way; I just didn't know how or when it was coming, so I just kept looking for the cloud the size of a man's hand.

One day as I was standing, I looked up and it was all over but the shouting. The great thing about it all was that I was still standing, but this time standing from a place of victory! *Hallelujah!*

When the Israelites took the city of Jericho, the Bible says:

> *On the seventh day, they got up at daybreak and marched around the city seven times in the same manner, except that on that day they circled the city seven times. The seventh time around, when the priests sounded the trumpet blast, Joshua commanded the army, "Shout! For the Lord has given you the city!"* (Joshua 6:15-16 NIV)

Then verse 20 continues:

> *When the trumpets sounded, the army shouted, and at the sound of the trumpet, when the men gave a loud shout, the wall collapsed; so everyone charged straight in, and they took the city. ...So the Lord was with Joshua, and his fame spread throughout the land* (Joshua 6:20,27 NIV).

My dear friend, rest in the faithfulness of God. He has never failed us, so, because of that, we don't have to give in to worry or be anxious, fearful, or depressed. When you are fighting for your *until* moment, you have to understand by faith that at any moment your situation could totally change for the better.

There is a wall that is getting ready to collapse in your very near future. You have to know that God has heard your prayer and you have to be ready to let out the biggest shout of your life because something is about to fall. The enemy wants you to magnify your problems and not magnify your God. But David said, *"Magnify the Lord"* because God is bigger—bigger than all the sickness, disease, failure, and disappointment.

Remember, the enemy comes to steal, kill, and destroy (see John 10:10). He wants to steal your peace and kill your joy and ultimately destroy you. Stress, sickness, and disease can rob you of your peace. God made our bodies to respond to emergency situations, but He gives joy in the midst of chaos.

Scientists refer to this as the "fight or flight" response. When facing stressors, our bodies have a built-in alarm system that mobilizes the body's resources for immediate physical activity. I have heard stories of unusual feats of physical strength in emergency situations, like having a burst of strength to lift an automobile when someone was trapped underneath. Or think of Elijah when he outran the chariot. It's quite amazing how God made our body systems to work together in dire situations. The heart rate increases and the muscle system kicks in; blood vessels adjust to give more blood to the brain and muscles while constricting flow to the skin; red blood cell production increases; the liver releases glycogen into the bloodstream for more energy; sweating increases to cool the body; respiratory passages widen to accommodate more oxygen; and certain enzymes and hormones are released.

Isn't it amazing how these systems all work together? These reactions will allow a person to run from danger or to conquer an enemy if needed. However, God made this to be temporary. If we are under prolonged stress or continual alarm, it will take a toll on our physical body. Stress (or distress) can cause fatigue, muscle aches and pains, digestive issues, heart palpitations, breathing difficulties, headaches, irritability, depression, and even lead to major diseases and death. But remember, God has called you to live in peace (see 1 Cor. 7:15).

A body at peace has a certain sound. The heart rate is normal, the blood pressure is normal, and all systems work in harmony. Scientists call this perfect state homeostasis. Think of a cat at peace and contented—it purrs. When a child calls out to their mom, that mother can discern by the sound of the child's voice whether it is a troubling cry or just a relational appeal.

Likewise, your *until* prayer has a certain sound to it. I have learned that it is very distinct to God and to you as well. Sometimes it's loud, and sometimes it's gentle and a quieting of the soul, but at the same time its power doesn't change. We should never equate the presence of God with a good mood or a pleasant temperament. God is near, whether you are happy or not.

Until prayer will require you to stand your ground and stay in peace to see your ultimate victory and see the devil defeated in your life. In order to see this accomplished, you must learn to avoid the stinkin' thinkin' and be determined to think God thoughts!

Your *Pray Until* Challenge

- Do you have a secret place where you can be with God until the storm passes?

- Remember Proverbs 10:25 says that when the storm passes the righteous will still be standing!

- What is the set pattern of prayer in your life and determination to have intimacy with the Lord?

Notes

1. Watchman Nee, *The Spiritual Man* (New York, NY: Christian Fellowship Publishers, Inc., 2014).

2. Rick Renner, *Sparkling Gems from the Greek II* (Tulsa, OK: Institute Books, 2016).

Chapter 12

THINKING UNTIL-
GOD THOUGHTS

And now, dear brothers and sisters, one final thing. Fix
your thoughts on what is true, and honorable, and right,
and pure, and lovely, and admirable. Think about things
that are excellent and worthy of praise.

—PHILIPPIANS 4:8 NLT

Endeavor to make good thought-choices. ...Line up your
thinking with the absolute truths of Scripture.

—SARAH YOUNG[1]

We live in the Information Age. Daily we are bombarded
with thoughts, suggestions, advertising, news (and fake
news), warnings, threats, weather reports, wars, and rumors of
wars—sound familiar? Psychologists claim humans have about
6,000 thoughts per day. That is about six and a half thoughts per
minute. That's a lot of neural synapses! No wonder we hear of brain
fog. These thoughts can be racing thoughts. They can be negative
thoughts. Hopefully, they are positive thoughts toward God,
our Creator.

What you take in by sight and sound will have an impact on your thoughts. A horror film may give you nightmares. A good testimony can give you hope. There are many Monday mornings I wake up with the previous day's worship songs still reverberating in my mind and spirit. Just like the television ad asks, "What's in your wallet?" I must ask, "What's in your mind or subconscious?" The old adage rings true: "Garbage in, garbage out."

How do we think God thoughts? Paul tells the Roman church to not conform to the world but to be transformed by renewing your mind, and he tells the Ephesian church to be renewed in the spirit of your mind (see Rom. 12:2; Eph. 4:23). Peter admonishes us to *"gird up the loins of your mind"* (1 Pet. 1:13). How? Well, the Word says, *"Let the word of Christ dwell in you richly in all wisdom, teaching and admonishing one another in psalms and hymns and spiritual songs, singing with grace in your hearts to the Lord"* (Col. 3:16).

Research has shown that people feel more positive after actively singing than they do after listening to music or talking about positive events. No wonder Paul said, *"I will sing with the Spirit, and I will sing with the understanding also"* (1 Corinthians 14:15b). Singing will affect your thoughts, your mind, your mood, and even your physical body. Advertisers know how to push all your emotional buttons. They know you will remember their jingle. How much better if we, like Paul, sing spiritual songs unto the Lord. I challenge you to make an effort to praise and worship daily, just like a dose of medicine. By focusing your thoughts on the Lord, it will be health to your body and nourishment to your bones (see Prov. 3:8). Paul explains in Philippians 4:7-8:

And the peace of God, which transcends all understanding, will guard your hearts and your minds in Christ Jesus. Finally, brothers and sisters, whatever is true, whatever is noble, whatever is right, whatever is pure, whatever is lovely, whatever is admirable—if anything is excellent or praiseworthy—think about such things (NIV).

Look at this: "If anything is excellent or praiseworthy." Then here is what you do: "Think *continually* on these things." As a matter of fact, center your mind on them and implant them in your heart. We must be able to fix our minds on the prize and on our great King and Lord:

Therefore, holy brothers and sisters, who share in the heavenly calling, fix your thoughts on Jesus, whom we acknowledge as our apostle and high priest (Hebrews 3:1 NIV).

Paul instructs us as well to:

Put on God's complete armor, that you may be able to resist and stand your ground on the evil day [of danger], and, having done all [the crisis demands], to stand [firmly in your place]. Stand therefore [hold your ground] (Ephesians 6:13-14 AMPC).

As we stand, we stand patiently and not just passively. Why? Because my stand is an act of aggression against every power of darkness because the last thing satan wants us to do is to stand. He wants us to quit, lay down, throw in the towel, and sit down on all the things that God has promised. But remember what God told the children of Israel when they were taking their territory:

Do not be afraid as you go out to fight your enemies today! Do not lose heart or panic or tremble before them. For the Lord your God is going with you! He will fight for you against your enemies, and he will give you victory! (Deuteronomy 20:3-4 NLT)

The enemy wanted us to abandon the miracle that we were believing for Kaylee. He wanted us to get tired, passive, become bitter and angry at God, and just to grow cool and eventually cold in our faith. The enemy saw her on meds the rest of her life. He envisioned her in some psych ward with padded walls, enduring counseling sessions the rest of her life. We saw her free, jumping and dancing on stage. We saw her writing songs and traveling around the world carrying this glorious Gospel and seeing people being set free just like she is doing now. Did I mention that God won? Hallelujah!

The greatest enemy of truth is silence. It seems as if the Church has lost its voice. We have lost our will to fight because of the fear and the sheer exhaustion of this culture that has bombarded us with political correctness, healthcare reform, the radical abortion agenda, discrimination and racism, and the list goes on. Our thoughts tend to be, in some strange way, mellowed out and jaded, but Paul so boldly declared:

For the grace of God that bringeth salvation hath appeared to all men, teaching us that, denying ungodliness and worldly lusts, we should live soberly, righteously, and godly, in this present world; looking for that blessed hope, and the glorious appearing of the great God and our Saviour Jesus Christ (Titus 2:11-13).

One of the reasons people love to go to amusement parks is because of the very meaning of the word *amused*. It literally means "not thinking." That makes plenty of sense when you see people aimlessly walking around in some amusement park, eating their favorite cotton candy. Yes, it sounds good to me too! People want to do something that will help them forget all the things that are weighing them down—hence, "amused, not thinking."

When you consider the tongue and all the things that the apostle James addresses about it in James 3, it is plain to see that there is definitely a connection between what you think, what you say, and how it affects you and the people around you. It would appear that we are simply *not thinking* about what we say and how it affects our lives. An Arab proverb says, "The mouth should have three gatekeepers: Is it true? Is it kind? Is it necessary?"

That's why we should think before we speak. I will even be so brave as to say, before you post something on social media, ask yourselves those three questions in light of making sure your brother or sister will not be offended or stumble.

Words are so powerful and they carry such a tremendous amount of weight. Jesus was very frank about words when He said:

Let me tell you something; Every one of these careless words is going to come back to haunt you. There will be a time of Reckoning. Words are powerful; take them seriously. Words can be your salvation. Words can also be your damnation (Matthew 12:36-37 MSG).

As you know, God used His creative power to *speak* the worlds into existence. Now that same spirit has been deposited into our spirit; therefore, we are creating the world that we inhabit by our words. In believing for your *pray until* moment, I can't describe to you how important your words are when you are contending. We cannot afford to be silent, but we must speak life words to our situations and not death. We must discern when to speak up and when to be quiet. James says:

> *My dear brothers and sisters, take note of this: Everyone should be quick to listen, slow to speak and slow to become angry* (James 1:19 NIV).

There is a miracle in your mouth, a victory in your voice. Because when you release your faith words out of your mouth, you are believing that whatever you say with your mouth and believe in your heart, it shall and will come to pass. This mountain that is before you has to be cast into the sea. The power of your God-given imagination enlarges you. It empowers you to live above this sin-infested world.

There is a process that God will bring you through when you are walking out your *pray until* moments. John the Baptist was very familiar with it. The process is called a wilderness. God took John into the wilderness so that he could find his voice, his message, his instructions, and his "what's next." There is no getting around it—you have to go to the wilderness to find your voice for this season. Most of the time, to produce the right words, the God thoughts, it will require the solitude and forsakenness of the wilderness.

You may ask, "What is a wilderness, Judy?" A wilderness by definition is a place where few people dwell, primarily because conditions are not conducive to the everyday lifestyle of most people. It is a place of loneliness, confinement, personal inconvenience, social ostracization and even unfriendly surroundings. When God gets ready to begin a work in our lives, we feel as if it is a wilderness, but He promises:

The desert and the parched land will be glad; the wilderness will rejoice and blossom. Like the crocus, it will burst into bloom; it will rejoice greatly and shout for joy. The glory of Lebanon will be given to it, the splendor of Carmel and Sharon; they will see the glory of the Lord, the splendor of our God (Isaiah 35:1-2 NIV).

When we were believing for our breakthrough with Kaylee, there was a very tight zip on our lips. I felt like I couldn't say anything about anything. God had both of us tied up like a knot with regard to talking. We were even careful of the people whom we allowed to speak into us because we were concerned that there would be opportunities for negativity to be spoken about Kaylee. We didn't want anything to have an adverse effect on our faith. James continues:

Those who consider themselves religious and yet do not keep a tight rein on their tongues deceive themselves, and their religion is worthless (James 1:26 NIV).

James pulls no punches when it comes to how we are to conduct ourselves concerning our thoughts, what we say and how we say it. Oswald Chambers said in *My Utmost for His Highest*: "Sometimes God puts us through the experience and discipline of darkness to teach us to hear and obey Him."

God always comes to the deep and utter recesses of our souls to speak to us. One of the many ways is through our God-given conscience. When the Holy Spirit comes, He will convict people of their sin (see John 16:8).

The conscience is the eye of the soul, which looks out either toward God or toward what we regard as the highest standard. Our conscience is something that God will use along with the sweet Holy Spirit to bring conviction for the things that make God sad. In other words, if I continually hold God's standard in front of me, my conscience will always direct me to God's perfect Word and instruct me in what I really should do. The question then becomes, will I obey? Your conscience is the part of your personality that helps you determine what is right and what is wrong. It is what makes you feel guilty when you do something bad, and good when you do something that is kind.

God hard wired us with an awareness of what is right and wrong and with an inclination to do what is right. So when the Holy Spirit comes, He will often speak to us by an inner witness.

> *The plans of the mind and orderly thinking belong to man, but from the Lord comes the [wise] answer of the tongue* (Proverbs 16:1 AMPC).

I should be able to live in such a renewed mind that I may be able to quickly "*prove what is that good, and acceptable, and perfect, will of God*" (Rom. 12:2).

I know for a fact that we can train our minds to think and talk in a manner that lines up with the Word of God. The Bible says that Jesus:

Though he were a Son, yet learned he obedience by the things which he suffered (Hebrews 5:8).

Jesus had to learn some things, even being God Himself; and believe me when I tell you that if Jesus had to learn obedience, we will have to learn obedience as well. Isaiah declared:

Thou wilt keep him in perfect peace, whose mind is stayed on thee: because he trusteth in thee (Isaiah 26:3).

Proverbs 12:25 says, "*Worry weighs a person down; an encouraging word cheers a person up*" (NLT).

It's very simple—keep your eyes and your thoughts on Him and you will live in peace. Remember that you can't allow yourself to annul what you are speaking and declaring in the spirit realm by also speaking out words of unbelief that your flesh may be tempted to release. Tell your flesh to shut up and tell your mind, will, and emotions to line up! Why? Because life and death is in the power of your tongue. So choose life and live or choose death and die (see Prov. 18:21). Solomon said:

All the ways of a man are pure in his own eyes, but the Lord weighs the spirits (the thoughts and intents of the heart) (Proverbs 16:2 AMPC).

Then verse 3 adds:

Roll your works upon the Lord [commit and trust them wholly to Him; He will cause your thoughts to become agreeable to His will, and] so shall your plans be established and succeed.

Observe what James says:

For we all often stumble and fall and offend in many things. And if anyone does not offend in speech [never says the wrong things], he is a fully developed character and a perfect man able to control his whole body and to curb his entire nature (James 3:2 AMPC).

James continues in verses 5 and 6 by saying:

And so the tongue is a small part of the body yet it carries great power! Just think of how a small flame can set a huge forest ablaze. And the tongue is a fire! It can be compared to the sum total of wickedness and is the most dangerous part of the human body. It corrupts the entire body and is a hellish flame! It releases a fire that can burn throughout the course of human existence (TPT).

In the original Aramaic the tongue *carries great power* and it *has dominion*. The thought also conveys that it will burn throughout generations. In other words, your children and your children's children can be affected by the words that flow from your mouth.

He continues by saying in verse 8, "*It's a fickle, unrestrained evil that spews out words full of toxic poison!*" (TPT). Now, here comes the great news:

But the wisdom from above is always pure, filled with peace, considerate and teachable. It is filled with love and never displays prejudice or hypocrisy in any form and it always bears the beautiful harvest of righteousness!

Good seeds of wisdom's fruit will be planted with peace-ful acts by those who cherish making peace (James 3:17-18 TPT).

In this verse, wisdom is always pure and holy. Then it becomes teachable, which is the concept of being easy to correct and ready to be convinced or willing to yield to others. As you read this chapter, I believe there is a wisdom that is coming straight from God to navigate you through this season when you need wisdom to be able to discern the plans of God. Again, James says:

If you need wisdom, ask our generous God, and he will give it to you. He will not rebuke you for asking (James 1:5 NLT).

When you think God thoughts, you will become what you think. Look at this powerful scripture: *"For as he thinketh in his heart, so is he"* (Prov. 23:7). When I read this passage I am reminded of what the spies called themselves when they went to spy out the land. *"We even saw giants there, the descendants of Anak. Next to them we felt like grasshoppers"* (Num. 13:33 NLT). And that's what they thought too!

You have to be careful what you call yourself. We are not a victim of our circumstances. We were created in the image of God, full of grace and power. The voices you allow into your mind and emotions are the feelings determining your present reality and ultimately your legacy. It could be movies, books, people, and especially stinkin' thinkin'! When we are overwhelmed with situations that occur in our lives, it's usually because we are allowing the voice of the enemy a foothold into our minds and spirits.

Dr. Robert Gay, in his book *Voices: Hearing and Discerning When God Speaks*, goes into depth of how to distinguish the voice of the Lord from the many other voices that we encounter on a daily basis. He says:

> The voice of emotion is the voice of feelings. Although God created our emotions, the voice of emotion was never intended to be the ruling voice within our lives. Emotion must be subjugated to the will and spirit of man. If the voice of emotion is given the helm of your ship, it will lead you astray.
>
> Emotion will naturally respond to the environment. It reacts to the actions and feelings of others. It is the part of you that is sensitive to how things are said more than what was said. It is the feelings center of your human makeup.
>
> It can easily be argued that the emotions have the loudest voice within you. While the spirit of man is the still small voice, emotion is the loudest and most impressive voice you experience.
>
> Regardless of what the feeling may be, the emotions shout. Unfortunately, the voice of emotion can hinder correct hearing and decisions. They can cloud the arena of your life with smoke that makes it difficult to see clearly and navigate.[2]

We can't allow the enemy to use our mind and emotions as a playing field to keep us in constant fretting and worrying. Instead, we have been given power through hearing our Shepherd's voice, the name of Jesus, the blood of Jesus, the power of His Word, the prayer of agreement, communion, fasting, and a thousand other things that God has placed in our arsenal of weapons. Paul said it best when he said:

Casting down imaginations, and every high thing that exalteth itself against the knowledge of God, and bringing into captivity every thought to the obedience of Christ (2 Corinthians 10:5).

"How do you think God thoughts to train your mind to think God thoughts?" you may ask. By knowing that He is worthy of all our confidence and worthy of all of our trust. Don't get me wrong—certainly there are people who deserve some of our confidence and some of our trust, but only God deserves *all of it!* The world we live in is increasingly unsafe and unpredictable, but God is the rock that provides us with a firm foundation for our life. So because of that, we take refuge as Psalm 18:2 admonishes us:

The Lord is my rock, my fortress, and my savior; my God is my rock, in whom I find protection. He is my shield, the power that saves me, and my place of safety (NLT).

Don't let your circumstances define your sense of peace and security. It is natural for us to want to be in control of our lives, but God can empower us to live supernaturally! The joy that He gives, the world didn't give it to you, and the world can't take it away. His joy transcends your circumstances.

Here is a prayer to pray concerning your thoughts and words.

Holy Spirit,
Put a watch over my mouth and convict me to use my words in a most uplifting way for Your purpose. I

believe, as Your Word declares, Your purposes and your plans will prevail (Prov. 19:21), which means no gossiping, no passing on of rumors, no whining, no complaining, no fear, doubt, or unbelief, no tearing myself down or others.

I declare with all humility and boldness that my tongue will not be set on fire from hell (James 3:2-10). I will instead make it my business as a believer to call forth those things which be not as though they are. I do this by repentance, renewing my conversation, finding a new way to express myself, thinking God thoughts from His Word, and breaking old patterns of speech that have held me back.

I boldly declare that God is my helper and I will follow His lead, and then my life will be filled with His love and blessing. In Jesus' name. Amen!

Now that we have come this far I want to remind you that the waters you are swimming in are deep waters, and your enemy is afraid of the deep things of God. But I must caution you, before we finish up, to watch out for the undercurrents. Let's keep swimming!

Your *Pray Until* Challenge

- Form a habit of doing something different during this season. Habits are hard to break, especially God habits!

- Don't ask the way when you know perfectly well the way. Just do it! No procrastination!

- How will you know when you have arrived at a certain destination? When a crisis comes up unexpectedly and you go instinctively to Him. That is how!

Notes

1. Sarah Young, *Jesus Always* (Nashville, TN: Thomas Nelson, 2018), 260.
2. Robert Gay, *Voices: Hearing and Discerning When God Speaks* (Tabor, SD: Parsons Publishing House, 2021).

Chapter 13

THE UNDERCURRENTS: THE OTHER SIDE OF UNTIL

Not that I have already obtained all this, or have already arrived at my goal, but I press on to take hold of that for which Christ Jesus took hold of me. Brothers and sisters, I do not consider myself yet to have taken hold of it. But one thing I do: Forgetting what is behind and straining toward what is ahead, I press on toward the goal to win the prize for which God has called me heavenward in Christ Jesus.

—PHILIPPIANS 3:12-14 NIV

God shapes the world by prayer. The more praying there is in the world, the better the world will be, the mightier the forces against evil.

—E.M. BOUNDS, *Purpose in Prayer*

Until has a sound. Sometimes it's loud and sometimes it's quiet while at the same time its power doesn't diminish.

—JUDY J. TUTTLE

As I'm writing this chapter, I am sitting on the beach in a beach chair under an umbrella sipping on a glass of iced tea.

Everything looks so nice and calm, but there is a red flag that is waving near the lifeguard stand. The red flag is warning everybody on the beach that they are not allowed to swim in the ocean because of a high hazard. Usually, it means there are very strong waves, undercurrents, or riptides, or maybe even some sharks have been spotted. In essence, what you are looking at may not seem dangerous, but it really is. The beautiful waves look so inviting to surf in, play in, and have fun in with your beach toys, but what you really should understand is that there is another side you can't see. There is something lurking, ready to take you under in a flash, and that is an undercurrent.

As it is in the natural, so it is in the spiritual—there is an enemy that we can't always see lurking to stop us, discourage us, and to ultimately defeat us. If we understand who he is and what his agenda is for our lives, then we can navigate through it more smoothly with the sword of the Spirit by our side. Peter warns us:

> *Be sober, be vigilant; because your adversary, the devil, as a roaring lion, walketh about, seeking whom he may devour* (1 Peter 5:8).

What I am referring to is the other side of your until moment. Sometimes when we gain a victory, we let our guard down, and if we are not careful and attentive the enemy will slip in through another outlet or through an unexpected turn of events. Here's the warning that Jesus gave:

> *When an evil spirit leaves a person, it goes into the desert, seeking rest but finding none. Then it says, "I will return to the person I came from." So it returns and finds its former home empty, swept, and in order. Then the spirit*

finds seven other spirits more evil than itself, and they all enter the person and live there. And so that person is worse off than before (Matthew 12:43-45 NLT).

Here are the facts:

- We live in a fallen world since Adam and Eve.
- We fight a very real enemy and his name is deceiver, liar, blasphemer, and accuser. He is satan, the devil himself.
- And I might add, he is a defeated foe.

When you gain a victory and do a victory lap, the enemy always is standing by waiting to trip you up again. Be very careful to keep your heart guarded, stay in church, stay in fellowship with other believers, and as Paul says:

Whoever thinks he is standing secure should take care not to fall (1 Corinthians 10:12 NABRE).

One of the pitfalls of the enemy is to get you tripped up thinking that, as they say in the south, "You have it made in the shade." But I would tell you, never let your guard down for the enemy to see where you are most vulnerable. If you start to neglect the most important things in your life that got you to your victory, you will be ensnared for the enemy to capture your thoughts again.

Jesus warned us that we would experience pressure. Rest assured, God is always in control when everything around you screams that He is not. It is true that bad things happen to good people and even God's people. Don't believe me? Read Job. How about Hebrews 11, "The Hall of Fame of Faith"?

Still others had trial of mockings and scourgings, yes, and of chains and imprisonment. They were stoned, they were sawn in two, were tempted, were slain with the sword. They wandered about in sheepskins and goatskins, being destitute, afflicted, tormented—of whom the world was not worthy (Hebrews 11:36-38 NKJV).

Pastor Jack Hayford expounds on this passage, saying:

The fact that others were tortured and suffered in various other ways indicates that faith does not provide an automatic exemption from hardships, trials, or tragedy. Furthermore, the experience of such difficulties does not mean that the people undergoing them possessed less faith than those who are not afflicted. The same faith that enables some to escape trouble enables others to endure it. The same faith that delivers some from death enables others to die victoriously. Faith is not a bridge over troubled waters, but is a pathway through them.

Discerning the pathway and the source of any hardships encountered requires aggressive prayer and worship. Through these means, God's perspective becomes focused. [1]

In actuality, there will be times in your *until* moments when it seems and feels and actually looks like the enemy has won and our Redeemer has failed, but Micah 7:8 declares:

Do not gloat over me, my enemies! For though I fall, I will rise again. Though I sit in darkness, the Lord will be my light (NLT).

We understand that God is working all things out for our good, and even in the midst of the undercurrents He still controls the winds and the waves. When I refer to undercurrents, I am speaking of our enemy. He parades around as an angel of light and as a liar and deceiver to undermine and bring confusion. Where we thought we had gained a victory and in fact *had* gained a victory, he is still not finished.

This is evident from the very first book of the Bible where Adam and Eve were confronted with the devil who approached them in a conniving manner. He said to them, as he says to us, "Did God really say?" He is constantly accusing us before the Father and trying to make us doubt all the promises of God and even doubt what is in front of our face—namely, your faith coming into sight. On the outside, you have gained a victory, but on the flip side, something is not adding up. It's because he is coming at you from a different angle now. But we are not ignorant concerning his ways.

Such was the case with Kaylee. During her ordeal with the spirit of fear, she gained victory when she was baptized in the Holy Spirit. There was a joy, a calmness, and a peace of God that came over her, which was accompanied by intense moments of worship and being alone in the presence of God with her Bible and her guitar.

I can imagine satan, who was the ex-worship leader in Heaven, was enraged by her bold faith and newfound freedom. Therefore, he changed his tactics by coming at her from different perspectives she was not accustomed to before. That is what I want to warn you about—satan is always in pursuit.

Even Jesus faced this onslaught of the sly deceiver. He came after Jesus had experienced one of His greatest moments in His life, which was His baptism. The Bible says:

Then Jesus was led up by the Spirit into the wilderness to be tempted by the devil. And when He had fasted forty days and forty nights, afterward He was hungry (Matthew 4:1-2 NKJV).

Look at all the indirect ways that he came after Him. First, he tempted Him with bread knowing He was hungry after 40 days and nights without eating. Then he tried to persuade Jesus, the Holy Son of God, to worship him. Next, he tried to make Him look like a fool by telling him to jump off of a cliff, and he even quoted (misquoted) scripture, but every time, Jesus counterattacked with the Word of God. Then the Bible says, *"When the devil had ended every temptation, he departed from Him until an opportune time"* (Luke 4:13 NKJV). In other words, satan said, "That didn't work, so I will have to come at Him from a different perspective, but I'll be back."

Kaylee was now wise to his shenanigans and she knew how to maneuver with the enemy coming straight *toward her.* When he would spew out the lies that she had heard time and time again, she knew what to do—quote those powerful scriptures. However, she was not accustomed to him coming behind her and hitting her in her knees, so to speak. She had to learn to distinguish all of the faces of his trickery and deception.

Now, instead of telling her she was going to die or tempting her to go and kill herself, he tried to convince her that she was not anointed, and that she was not a good singer or a good musician or other petty stuff to crush her. Is it a coincidence, or was the devil jealous of the very thing that was taken from him as the anointed cherub and musician? No, it wasn't a coincidence—he hated her worship, her beautiful aptitude in guitar, and he certainly hated her voice of worship.

So Kaylee had to be acquainted with the devil's voice and her Father's voice. She knew what the enemy's voice did to her spirit and her emotions. So she had to learn to distinguish between the two, because they were his new undertows.

Paul had to address this very thing when he and Silas were being followed by a young girl possessed by a demon:

> *One day as we were going to the place to pray, we met a servant-girl who could tell what was going to happen in the future by a demon she had. Her owner made much money from her power. She followed Paul and us crying out, "These are servants of the Highest God. They are telling you how to be saved from the punishment of sin." She did this many days. Paul was troubled. Then he turned and said to the demon in her, "In the name of Jesus Christ, I speak to you. Come out of her!" At once it left her* (Acts 16:16-18 NLV).

On the outside looking in, it would seem as if this was something good that this young girl was doing, but the fact of the matter was, she was an undercurrent. This demon wasn't praising and magnifying God; it was using this young girl to be cynical, deceiving, cunning, and really trying to expose Paul and Silas' real agenda in spreading the Gospel of Jesus. The demon spirit was actually trying to get them in trouble, as it did later on with the girl's owner, who had them thrown into prison.

Paul probably at first thought that the demon would subside and get worn down from being ignored, but Paul had one of those

"I can't take it anymore!" moments. Paul decided, "I have heard his mouth long enough, and this young girl has been enslaved long enough, and it's time for a change!" Paul may have even discerned what was probably going to be next as a result of exposing this demonic activity. But he also knew, at the end of the day, he just couldn't take it anymore!

How about you? Are you at the end of the end? Have you had enough of what the devil is doing to your life, your family, your future, your mind? Are you at an *until* moment of your life when something has got to change and you are tired of his mouth? The undercurrent of the enemy wants you to cave and doubt all the promises of God and all the prophecies spoken over your life and the lives of the people you love. He senses something wonderful is ahead and he shudders to think that his plans will fail. What I know is that God's plans always prevail. One of my favorite scriptures is Jeremiah 29:11:

> *"For I know the plans I have for you," declares the Lord, "plans to prosper you and not to harm you, plans to give you hope and a future"* (NIV).

Hebrews encourages us to:

> *Persevere so that when you have done the will of God, you will receive what he has promised* (Hebrews 10:36 NIV).

What I have learned is that we can actually outlast the devil. We can ignore his tactics and he can become frustrated and leave us as he did Jesus, and he will be forced to look for another opportune time. Remember:

The eternal God is your refuge, and underneath are the everlasting arms; He will thrust out the enemy from before you, and will say, "Destroy!" (Deuteronomy 33:27 NKJV)

Miracles go against all the natural laws, but here is the crux of the matter—when you take miracles out of your life, you take the whole of Christianity out of your life! Christianity began because of a man called Jesus who rose from the dead! You can't throw in the towel in the face of your miracle. If it's a big deal to you, it's a big deal to God. If you seek miracles, you probably won't find them, but if you seek the Giver of the miracles, then miracles will find you.

My mom came from a family who loved God and was devoted to Him and His Church. My Aunt Belle, her older sister, died from breast cancer fairly young at the age of 52 and she left behind 15 children. They all loved my mama with such a deep love because their mom and my mom were very close, so we all had a lot in common. They gave her the name Aunt Gay, short for Gaynell.

I remember one particular year, it was the end of summer, and my mom inquired of my dad if there was any possible way that she could go and visit with my cousin Evelyn in New York who was dying with breast cancer. She also was at a young age. Even though there were lots of things to do at the end of the summer, my dad agreed for my mom to go and be with her.

She traveled by bus all by herself on a 12-hour-long journey to New York to be with her precious niece and to probably say her goodbyes. I know for a fact my mom took her bottle of oil, a prayer cloth that our church had prayed over, and of course she was fasting and praying as well.

When she arrived, it was unfortunately worse than what she was told. Yes, she was in her last days here on earth. My mom stayed with her in the hospital room from the moment she arrived until her death. Not long after her arrival, the doctor informed the family that it wouldn't be long before she would be gone. As she sat there by her bedside, holding Evelyn's hand, she was praying, consoling, and singing over her. There seemed to be so much peace in the room with the family surrounding her.

All at once, Evelyn began to cry out to my mom, "Make him get out of here, Aunt Gay. There he is, make that devil leave."

My mom knew the schemes of the evil one; he was there at the very end, just to torture her. The Bible says the last enemy to be destroyed is death itself (see 1 Cor. 15:25). My mom said to Evelyn, "Listen to me, honey, repeat this prayer after me: 'Our Father who art in Heaven, hallowed be Thy name.'" When she started saying the Lord's Prayer, all of a sudden the peace of God came into the room, and in just a few moments, with a smile on her face and peace in her heart, she went to meet her Lord. The devil was there to the very end, but so was Jesus in great power! He kept His promise to Evelyn when He said "though I walk through the valley of the shadow of death, I will fear no evil for thou art with me."

Your battle is not:

Against flesh and blood, but against principalities, against powers, against the rulers of the darkness of this age, against spiritual hosts of wickedness in the heavenly places (Ephesians 6:12 NKJV).

Again, he is a defeated foe. There is one thing you can depend on. The Word says:

When you pass through the waters, I will be with you; and through the rivers, they shall not overflow you. When you walk through the fire, you shall not be burned, nor shall the flames scorch you. For I am the Lord your God, the Holy One of Israel, your Savior (Isaiah 43:2-3 NKJV).

Your God is fighting for you and the fight is always fixed. Am I telling you that there have not been any more battles with Kaylee? Absolutely not! There will always be a fight—another fear to whisper in all of our ears trying to convince us of who we are *not*. I love the fact that Paul said:

None of the rulers of this age understood it [the plan of salvation], *for if they had, they would not have crucified the Lord of glory* (1 Corinthians 2:8 NIV).

That lets you know what an idiot the devil is. So, no worries! As a matter of fact, go ahead and strike out to the beach. I hear the water is great! Now let's sum up the whole reason for this book.

Your *Pray Until* Challenge

- Have you ever had to really hold tightly to what God promised when all seems lost and the opposite of what you are believing God for is happening?

- Was there a time when things looked good on the surface, but by the spirit you sensed something was off or even dreadfully wrong? Is that time right now?

- Can you see beyond the person who seems so evil and really understand that the enemy is the real culprit?

Note

1. Jack Hayford, *The New Spirit Filled-Life Bible* (Nashville, TN: Thomas Nelson, 2013), Notes.

Chapter 14

THE WHY OF UNTIL

Now to Him who is able to do exceedingly abundantly above all that we ask or think.
—EPHESIANS 3:20 NKJV

This is not a time to be down, discouraged, disappointed or depressed. It's show time for God! It's testimony time to decree and declare and demonstrate His mighty power. He saves the Best for Last!
—UNKNOWN

W hy *Pray Until?* Why would you pick up a book like this and put yourself through so much agony of soul to see something change in someone else's life? After all, if they make their bed hard, shouldn't they just lie in it? If it is a situation typical of a generation in your family, is it going to make a difference? Why? Why pray until?

You may find yourself in so many scenarios in this thing called life, and from day to day you never know what it will throw at you. One minute everything is peachy, and the next minute all hell has broken out. What do you do when everything that can be shaken is now shaking, rattling, and rolling? One thing you do is stay rooted and grounded in the unshakable Word of God, and know that He is in total control. After you pray and believe what He said is truth, then you give Him thanks and wait expectantly for the answer to manifest. The psalmist said:

In the morning, Lord, you hear my voice; in the morning I lay my requests before you and wait expectantly (Psalm 5:3 NIV).

Expectation is the key to getting believing prayers answered. Your confidence is not in your prayers, but in the God who answers prayers. Paul instructs us to:

Be anxious for nothing, but in everything by prayer and supplication, with thanksgiving, let your requests be made known to God (Philippians 4:6 NKJV).

That's where pastors Josh and Nadine Bowles found themselves—in a very shaky place where it felt like the bottom had not only dropped out, but there was no landing place in sight.

They came to us tired, broken, and hurting from being in some places where they had been laboring, and quite honestly they just needed a sabbatical. They moved to Cleveland, Tennessee, and started attending our church, Dwelling Place Church International. We loved them from moment one, and wanted them to feel our love and support. Along with Benny, their three-year-old, they just needed some down time, and we gave it to them. We sort of nursed them back to vitality by allowing them just to be a family again and to enjoy just coming to church and sitting under ministry. After a couple of years, they became our young student pastors.

They were enjoying tremendous success, and they were a blessing to our lives.

Josh and Nadine were both Rhema College graduates, and to say they knew the Word was an understatement. They lived, slept, and ate the Word. Pastor Josh was and still is one of the most powerful preachers I know and a very prolific and gifted young man. Nadine as well has loved Jesus her entire life and dedicated her whole self to the cause of Christ in addition to being a faithful wife and a wonderful mother.

They both believed in the power of prayer, and not just any prayer. They believed in bold, courageous, and audacious prayer. They lived faith, talked faith, and walked in faith. They were a blessing and delight to be around. But things were getting ready to change; they would meet eye to eye with *until* prayer and the *why* of it.

Here is their story.

We were so excited to find out our family of three was being upgraded to four. May 24, 2013 we found out the news that we were expecting another baby. What we weren't expecting, however, was the fight it would take to walk in the fullness of that blessing. After a relatively perfect pregnancy with our first son, I didn't know the hardship that so many others had experienced, from morning sickness all the way to receiving life-threating news about your child's health.

At a routine prenatal ultrasound in September 2013, we found out we were having a boy. We were so excited for Ben, our oldest, to have a brother for life. During the ultrasound they also found two large cysts on the baby's head. They weren't terribly concerned, as they said these things sometimes work themselves out without any problems, but it could be an indicator of other issues. A follow-up appointment was scheduled for a few weeks later, and we went home.

This initial news of the cysts wasn't necessarily life-threatening to our son, but as a mother, there's something in you that rises up to war against any perceived danger, even when your child is in utero. I remember getting home from that appointment, sitting down on my bed and praying a simple prayer. I believed, and had for a long time, that God was a healer. I had witnessed it firsthand. But I still asked Him to point me in the right direction in His Word. I knew His Word was the final authority and I wanted Him to show me in the Word of God where to stand. As soon as that prayer left my mouth, I haphazardly flipped open my Bible and my eyes immediately landed in Psalm 147. There were no verses in that chapter underlined at that time, but it was as if the Holy Spirit was circling and highlighting verse 13 with neon lights. "For He strengthens the bars of your gates; He blesses your children within you."

The immediate joy and peace I found myself in was glorious. It's hard to put into words how amazing it is to hear the still, small-yet-dynamic voice of the Author of life. His Word told me that He had blessed this son I was carrying, and what He blesses, no enemy can curse. I sensed the strengthening in faith and immediately received His Word as the greater truth for our son and his outcome. There was no talking me out of it; I knew at that next appointment, those cysts would not be an issue.

That tiny moment on my bed that afternoon was a small but important victory in my faith walk. It certainly wasn't the first time I had sought God and heard His voice. But hearing some potentially bad news about our unborn son was working some faith muscles in a way I hadn't had to previously, at least not to the same intensity. Seeking God in prayer, receiving His Word, and believing what God says isn't terribly complex, but when it directly contradicts the ultrasound picture lying beside you, it does require faith. Some staying power. Some guts. Some grit.

Little did I know that day's faith exercise was really more like a light warm-up to the serious weight lifting ahead.

When I was 20 weeks pregnant, at our follow-up appointment the ultrasound technician gave us the good news that the cysts were completely gone. I beamed in great thankfulness to our good God. Although I was quickly sobered by the puzzled look and careful prodding of the technician who continued to scan the rest of our son's body. After a long time of silence, she gave me new news. It looked like the baby's heart was on the wrong side of the body. They immediately sent me to the high-risk doctor that afternoon for further testing.

The 30-minute car ride to the Chattanooga doctor was another battlefield. I called my husband, Josh, at work and told him the news so he could meet me at the appointment. After we hung up, I began talking to Jesus as if He was sitting next to me. I was so excited God had answered my prayer about the cysts, but I felt a little stunned by the news about his heart. What was going on? How could this be happening? It's not what I imagined. I was hoping for what I experienced the first time—a plain, uneventful, healthy pregnancy. I wasn't cut out for this. I had trusted Him, but now there was more trouble. I felt my confidence shake a bit. As I poured out by heart to Him with tears, I heard His voice again. It was as if He was sitting right beside me in the car. In His gentle, beautiful way He said, "Nadine, this is the confidence you can have in Me. If you ask anything according to My Word, I hear you. And if I hear you, you will have whatever you ask of Me." He was speaking First John 5:14-15 directly to me, a verse I had stored away in my heart as a child but so desperately needed at that moment.

That moment in the car is where our second son's name originated. Samuel means "the Lord hears," and after I parked the car, a calm and steady strength rose up in me. I knew God was listening to me. I paid close attention to how He responded to my cries of fear, complaint, and urgency. The key to answered prayer would be prayer according to His Word. If I could find out what He said, what He thinks about things, I would be agreeing with an omniscient God who is known for miracles. To be heard by such a powerful and good God would give confidence even in the darkest battle.

At the high-risk doctor, they diagnosed Samuel's condition as Congenital Diaphragmatic Hernia (CDH). I had never heard of it and was reluctant to find out more. The condition meant there was a half-dollar sized hole in his diaphragm, allowing the abdominal organs to migrate into the chest. When this happens, it doesn't leave enough space for lungs to develop, making it hard for the baby to breathe. At this point, they were unable to determine just how much of his stomach contents had drifted, but the mass was enough to push his heart to the wrong side of the body. Our doctor was tender but truthful as he shared the possible outcomes of this condition. Fifty percent of children diagnosed survive. Most all of the survivors have some sort of long-term health issue.

While there was an experimental surgery offered to certain patients with this condition, we did not qualify. We soberly left the doctor that day and felt shocked. None of this was what we expected. There was a long list of appointments for the next three months leading up to his birth, and seeing it all at once felt overwhelming. With no medical background, barely being able to pronounce most of the words in the literature they provided I could hardly see myself fighting this battle victoriously. I did not feel qualified to fill this role.

In the days that followed, my husband and I were diligent and desperate to do everything we could to prepare for Sam's arrival. We were blessed to already have the arsenal of equipment and supplies needed for a newborn. But we set our heart, mind, and strength to prepare in the spirit for his coming. We dove into the Word of God like never before and saturated ourselves with every faith-filled teaching on healing. We surrounded ourselves with people of faith who radically believed God and had victoriously walked through their battles. Whenever sleepless nights would come—either due to physically being uncomfortable with my growing belly or my mind trying to entertain some worrying thoughts—I would read through the Psalms. I found so much comfort there. It was such a special time when God was so actively and gently speaking. Every time a scripture spoke directly, I copied it down in a note in my phone.

A rich and deep trail of truth began developing, not just in that phone note page but in my heart. Hearing the Word, meditating on it, and speaking it back to God became the most important and regular parts of our day. It wasn't just one time a day, but all throughout the day. "Praying at all times in the Spirit with all kinds of prayer" was where you could find us. The passage in Ephesians 6 where we're instructed to pray like that (Eph. 6:18a) is commanding us to prepare spiritually like a soldier prepares for battle. If we were going to come out of this battle victorious, we would need to be armed and ready for opposition. And there was no shortage of it.

Information has such a powerful effect on us. What we put into our minds directly affects what we believe, and how we act stems from that. In order to walk in a faith that pleases God, we must get the first step right and be choosey about what we're thinking on. In our information age, when we can Google all our questions and find instant answers, we decided to pass up consulting the internet for more information on CDH. It may have been because we were scared to find out more. Already at our nearly weekly doctor's appointments we were hearing plenty of bad news. It was so easy to be discouraged after sitting through and hearing the prognosis, so we would always walk out of those doors ready to bombard our hearts with the good news. We made sure the good news was coming into our hearts and minds in larger quantities than the bad news. Looking back and knowing what I know now about CDH, I believe it was one of the best decisions we made to not look it up online.

I remember some well-loved and well-meaning friends offering prayers and their attempts at encouragement to us during this time. They implored us to trust God no matter what happened, softly implying that Sam might not make it. We had every intention to trust God—that was our lifeline at the time! We had settled that God was not to be blamed for anything, but it was up to us to be found doing what He instructed in His Word. Even though the probability of death was mentioned, I had dug my feet in and grounded myself on the truth that he would live and not die and declare the works of the Lord (Ps. 118:17); that with long life he would be satisfied, be shown the Lord's salvation (Ps. 91:16); that the

Lord heals all his diseases (Ps. 103:3); and that the Lord would perfect that which concerned me (Ps. 138:8).

Scripture had given me such a firm footing to stand on and was the whole basis of my faith. Faith in God begins where the will of God is known. Through many scriptures, the Lord was faithful to speak His will about Sam, and we trusted that if we were found believing, He would be faithful to perform His Word. In the case of healing, God answered my prayer to show me in the Word where to stand, and He made His will perfectly clear—that He was willing and able to heal, and He ultimately did it on the cross! I wasn't trying to beg or plead or twist God's arm in this matter. If God didn't want healing to be part of His plan, He was under no obligation to add it. But if He so generously and graciously factored divine healing into His package of salvation, I was not going to let that benefit go unused. His blood was too precious to let this purchased gift lie dormant, and it was the very thing Sam needed.

Three months passed quickly, and on January 23, 2014 Samuel Patrick Bowles was born in a room full of scary-looking equipment and his 14-person medical team. God did so much that day in answered prayer. At the beginning of my pregnancy, my heart's desire was to have a simple, intimate delivery with a midwife. After Sam's diagnosis, those dreams were shattered as I would need to deliver in a hospital with a well-furnished NICU. When I met my nurse that day, she introduced herself as Christy Tullos and told us that in addition to being a labor and delivery nurse, she had just graduated with her certification in midwifery! God was so kind to fulfill even that little desire. She became a great friend and important source of encouragement and prayer our whole hospital stay.

The moment Sam was born, they scooped him up and laid him on my chest and my husband laid his hands on him and began to pray and bless him. The first thing those sweet little ears heard upon entry was the prayers of the saints. We didn't even have a chance to take a picture before they swooped him up and began working on intubating him.

We, and a whole network of prayer warriors, had prayed so much leading up to his birth. Those previous months I was living on the edge of expectation, just knowing that our miracle was about to surface. Many countless ultrasounds followed after his birth, but I had it all played out in my head how I would react when they told me my baby's body was perfectly restored to normal. It seemed like the perfect opportunity for God to show His display of power and wow the technicians. Yet every ultrasound went the same way—all 45 of them. That moment never came, and when disappointment would try and settle in, I would cling to First Peter 2:6: "Behold, I am laying in Zion a stone, a cornerstone chosen and precious, and whoever believes in Him will never be disappointed." Jesus was the rock I was standing and believing on. He was the basis for my faith in healing. He said I wouldn't be disappointed when trusting Him, but here I was, feeling a little impatient and let down by not seeing the answer yet. This whole process had so many variables that weren't in my planning, and perfect opportunities for disappointment and discouragement to set in. And yet First Peter 2:6 was staring me in the face and confronting the way I felt.

Choosing to believe God in those moments of disappointment felt risky. When you start speaking the Word, which is contrary to everything you see, it can even feel like you're lying. Your statement of faith can be completely opposite of what you're experiencing and can look small and foolish as well. Walking by faith and not by sight is not for the faint of heart. It's not for quitters. No wonder we're encouraged to "fight the good fight of faith" (1 Tim 6:12). Staying in faith takes some grit and stamina. It requires knocking down those thoughts of fear, doubt, and unbelief. This process had felt like a huge wrestling match to me, straining to believe God while being pushed on by my opponent. Struggling to stay on top. I became so impressed with the story of Jacob who endured a wrestling match with God. His relentless statement in Genesis 32:26 was something I had endeavored to imitate during my own journey. When he was told to let go he said, "I will not let go unless You bless me." That picture of holding on until the blessing/the promise/the manifestation of your prayers came was calling me to strength even in these weak moments.

Sam was put in the NICU at Vanderbilt Children's Hospital and decorated with all sorts of medical accessories.

It was overwhelming to step into his room the first time and see him lying alone in a box, tubes and stickers coming out of every section of his sweet, helpless body. In addition to being intubated, he was put under intense bilirubin lights due to his rising jaundice. His other numbers were overall stable, and while we were expecting healing for our baby boy, the doctors and nurses looked like they were preparing for an intense battle for his life. He was the only baby in a large room with a huge contraption next to him—an ECMO machine that would offer total life support to a struggling infant. It certainly seemed like overkill those first two days, but on day three of his life, Josh and I walked in at 8 a.m. to see our child surrounded by medical staff working to revive and stabilize him. To our horror, his vitals were crashing.

I can't put into words how awful it is to watch your kids struggle and suffer and not be able to help them. And I'm sure many of you know exactly what that is like. It goes against nature to not jump in and help and save your child. But there was nothing I could do in that moment except pray. And, thank God, that was more than enough.

It was so overwhelming to watch. While my husband stayed tucked into the corner of the room, I had to step out. I found a dark, empty room, stepped inside, and shut the door behind me. I couldn't believe what I was seeing. Through this whole process, I never once entertained the idea that Sam would die. I had heard it suggested, but I had never in my heart or mind played that idea out. I was clinging so wholeheartedly to God's promise, but suddenly I started to feel like I had made a mistake. A voice started speaking to me in that room that he was going to die and I was so foolish for being in denial over it. I was weeping as this massive defeat rushed over me. I couldn't believe it. That voice continued taunting me with the terrible, inevitable outcome.

But thank God for the Word.

When you're squeezed, what's inside of you will come out. In this pressing, dark moment, I found another voice that was louder, stronger, and more confident than the previous words I was hearing. Bubbling out of my spirit came the active, living, powerful Word of God saying with confidence, "He will live and not die and declare the works of the Lord"! Darkness dissipated and as I soaked once again in that truth that stood in stark contrast to what I had witness in that NICU room, I decided to believe it, and hold on to it no matter what.

Sam was stabilized that day, and the days that followed were spent letting his body rest for his upcoming corrective surgery. Every day, usually multiple times a day, when Sam's room was cleared by his medical team, we pulled out that note in my phone and began boldly declaring God's Word. One of the greatest definitions of faith I've heard is acting like God's Word is true. When you speak the Word of God with the attitude of faith, you are unlocking the mountain-moving faith that Jesus spoke of in Mark 11:23-24. We didn't see those mountains moving for Sam in a dramatic, instant way, but there were certainly some rumblings going on.

Even though Sam's corrective surgery was delayed three times, God worked it out to pair him up the day of surgery with one of the most experienced CDH surgeons in the field. During surgery, they gently pulled down all the organs that migrated into the chest and sewed the hole in the diaphragm shut. Doctors told us that every one of Sam's organs had shifted up except the liver, meaning his chest was very crowded. They determined he had more lung mass than expected—nearly a full lung on the right side and half a lung on the left.

Things continued improving, little by little each day. One by one over the next few weeks, Sam's extensive medical equipment disappeared one thing at a time. They were able to remove his breathing tube and replace it with a cannula. We were finally able to hear our baby boy's voice! The intubation tube made it impossible for him to make noise, even cry, and for the first time we heard him make his presence known. Crying never sounded so sweet! It was a sign that he was moving the right direction.

After he was strong enough to breathe on his own, another big milestone came—it was time for him to learn to eat. All these little achievements made me realize how much I had taken them for granted with our first son. Even though there were all sorts of negative predictions about his ability to eat, Sam demonstrated great ambition to overcome all obstacles. We were wanting so desperately to see the finished work of God in Sam's body, and yet improvement just seemed to be creeping along in small doses. What we didn't realize at the time was that long stretches of tiny blessings add up to one miraculous and great finish. Ordinary days can feel boring and unspectacular, although I have found God can do His best work there.

On February 24, exactly one month and one day after Sam's arrival, he was released to come home! It was a triumph supernaturally delivered, and it marked the closing of one of the most treacherous walks we'd ever encountered. It's awful to have your faith tested, but I couldn't deny that I had seen God work and speak so marvelously, and I wouldn't have traded it for anything.

When we got home, we were filled with so much gratitude for what the Lord had done. Holding Sam and seeing his body free from cords and tubes and monitors, eating and growing, free from any kind of medication or disability made me stand in awe of the goodness of Jesus. We had prayed, and God had answered. Every night before bed was a worship session and ended with us laying our hands on our boys and blessing them. It's one of my favorite things to do to speak God's desires over them.

One year later, God showed His power in another amazing way. As a CDH patient, Sam would continue to have routine x-rays to monitor his lung and organ development. We left the hospital with him having a lung and a half, and part of our nightly blessing was proclaiming that he had "two fully developed lungs." Along the way, doctors were pleased with how his heart and organs had drifted back to the correct spot all on their own. God had made order to the chaos inside this once jumbled body, and people were taking note. After his one-year x-ray exam back at Vanderbilt, the doctor came into our room holding a copy of the x-rays. He said he didn't know how, but Sam now had two fully developed lungs (his exact words!) and that if he didn't know Sam's medical history, he would have never known he ever had CDH!

All these years later, as we see Sam continue to thrive as the picture of health, we are still amazed and provoked to worship. God answers prayer. I realized that all those times during that season of feeling disappointed and let down and unheard just meant one thing—God wasn't finished and it wasn't the end. If we had given up hope and quit in the middle, we may have never known the extent of how God was able to bless. We have every reason to be confident in the God who hears and answers prayers when they're prayed according to His will. He perfected the thing that concerned us, and we live and breathe to know this marvelous God and share His goodness with the world.

Wow! What an amazing and faithful Father we serve. One of the reoccurrences over and over again in pastor Josh and Nadine's testimony is the fact that God kept speaking His Word, and they stood on it, and as a result, they saw every answer to prayer they petitioned for.

Why pray until? Because there is a little Samuel who is filled with the Holy Spirit and with the Word of God and his parents pour into him along with his big brother every day. He is a blessing to his family, to his church, and I believe one day very soon to the nations of the world.

Why pray until? There is always someone waiting for you. Somewhere in the future, God wants to take you where you've never been before. He wants to heal your marriage and restore your body and cause you to prosper in ways that will astound you. He wants to send revival to your church, your community, your home, and your nation. There is a son/daughter depending on you to never quit praying for them and to hold on to the unchanging and never dying Word of the Living God.

Why pray until? There is a Judith Kaylee depending on her mama and daddy to pray her through this devilish nightmare that will one day put her on stages only dreamed of in the spirit! Why pray until? Because there is a mama up in glory, Sister Gaynell Chavis Jacobs, who is enjoying the sons she prayed for, and those prayers lived on even while she was walking on the streets of glory!

That is the why! He is *the Why!* He will forever be *the Why!*

May the Lamb that was slain receive the reward of His suffering!

Don't stop—*until!*

Here is my prayer for you as you move toward seeing all your heart's desires answered:

I pray that out of his glorious riches he may strengthen you with power through his Spirit in your inner being, so that Christ may dwell in your hearts through faith. And I pray that you, being rooted and established in love, may have power, together with all the Lord's holy people, to grasp how wide and long and high and deep is the love of Christ, and to know this love that surpasses knowledge— that you may be filled to the measure of all the fullness of God (Ephesians 3:16-19 NIV).

Amen!

Afterword

Is It Going to Be Worth It?

By Kaylee Tuttle

I have typed and retyped this afterword about five times trying to process what I wanted to tell you. There are many things I could say and many stories I could tell. I could try to recall the bad days and express to you again that it won't be easy, even though my mom has already told you. I could even pull out the good days when I didn't have a panic attack or a depressive episode to stir your faith to push for the good days! But while praying for you, I felt the Holy Spirit wanted me to tell you why you push "until." He specifically said, "Just tell them *your* afterward." Ironic, huh? Will there be good and bad days? Sure. But to tell you those and to not mention the complete, overcoming, and overwhelming power of the blood of Jesus would cheapen my story and would cheapen the cross.

Let's just skip to the victory, shall we? After about six years of the battle, I had started to get desperate because I was becoming older and tired of the life I lived. I thought suicide, I thought drugs, I thought of a lot of other routes, and because of how I was raised none of those just seemed to be the fix. My parents' prayers, even though strong, no longer sustained me. So, I turned to the presence of God myself. I had acquired friends from our church who taught me how to pray. We'd get together to just pray for fun and they'd teach me, "Kaylee, if you ask Him to come, He will come." And boy, did He! It started to become easier to say no to fear and to resist depression. My life centered on getting in the presence of God after school. I'd spend hours on top of my shoes in my closet or in my bedroom screaming Jason Upton and Steffany Gretzinger lyrics. I didn't spend this time with Jesus because I wanted breakthrough. I spent this time because I fell in love with Him. I was overcome by a love that was greater than fear and a joy that couldn't be taken away because of that same love.

I remember when fear would peek its head in on certain days in high school and I'd go back in that prayer closet and thank God that I had been set free, despite my feelings and thoughts. I was in this beautiful story with the Lord for about a year and a half when I found myself at a prayer meeting in May 2012. I was 13 and was madly in love with Jesus. My parents' prayers got me to this point, but I was flying above every lie with Jesus on my own. I remember being at this prayer meeting and going through my usual "prayer list." In the beginning of my own "until" journey, I used to start out with thanksgiving and would just thank the Lord for setting me free from fear and depression (again, even on days when I still felt those things). But this specific time felt different. I began to mumble to myself, "You are so faithful, You are so faithful!" I repeated this over and over because it just rested in my spirit. Then it hit me. My reality of fear and depression suddenly became my past. My natural collided with the supernatural and I realized that instead of praising my way through, I had praised my way out. I sat on the floor on the left side, on the fourth row of our church and tried to recall the last time I felt fear...and couldn't remember. I tried to remember a thought I used to have that would send me in a depressed state...and couldn't.

What am I trying to tell you? I am almost 25 now, and my story is this—*whom the Son sets free is free indeed*. I no longer live in fear. I am the most joyful person I know. I am in full-time ministry with my family and live a very full life. I laugh at the smallest things, eat a lot (I didn't eat much at all in my battle!), make excuses to go have fun, have slumber parties with my best friends (yes, I'm 24), go on vacations with my family and actually have fun, and, honestly, just enjoy life. While I do these things, I also burn to see awakening. In you. Your kids. Your family. I want you to know Jesus rightly. He is not a pew on a Sunday morning. He is your Brother, Friend, Healer, Savior, and your God. He wants to come through for you and *will* come through for you.

Jonathan Edwards said, "God does nothing in the earth except in response to prayer." My life wouldn't be full without the love of Jesus but also wouldn't be where it is without a praying mother and father. They reckoned in themselves that seeing me laugh, love, have fun, and live a life completely unto the Lord would be worth it. They sacrificed who they were, invested time, tears, pain, and suffering for the sake of their kid. They counted the cost and today, fear is scared of me. It senses when I walk into a room and has to leave when I tell it to through the name of Jesus.

So I ask you this question. Will it be worth it? To see your baby laugh again. To feel your husband hold you again. To see your wife in her right mind—let my testimony be your answer. Yes, it will! I don't remember anything from that season. Actually, many of the stories told in this book I had to dig in my memory bank for and, truthfully, couldn't remember. He wipes the very thought of our past away. What the enemy meant for bad, God turned it around personally for me. Continue in the *until* or start it, but whatever you do, don't turn around or stop. Your *until* awaits.

> *God blesses those who patiently endure testing and temptation. Afterward they will receive the crown of life that God has promised to those who love him* (James 1:12 NLT).

ABOUT JUDY JACOBS

*J*udy Jacobs is known for her dynamic and inspiring international ministry. A singer, songwriter, worship leader, teacher, mentor, and sought-after conference speaker, she is the founder of His Song Ministries and the International Institute of Mentoring. Judy also co-pastors Dwelling Place Church International along with her husband, Pastor Jamie Tuttle. Together, they received the United States Presidential Lifetime Achievement Award for dedicating their lives to full-time ministry and community service. She has authored numerous books including *Take It by Force, Stand Strong, Don't Miss Your Moment, You Are Anointed for This*, and *Tapestry of Love*. Judy and her husband have two daughters, Kaylee and Erica, and reside in Cleveland, Tennessee.

YOUR Prophetic COMMUNITY

Are you passionate about hearing God's voice, walking with Jesus, and experiencing the power of the Holy Spirit?

Destiny Image is a community of believers with a passion for equipping and encouraging you to live the prophetic, supernatural life you were created for!

We offer a fresh helping of practical articles, dynamic podcasts, and powerful videos from respected, Spirit-empowered, Christian leaders to fuel the holy fire within you.

Sign up now to get awesome content delivered to your inbox
destinyimage.com/sign-up

Destiny Image